THE PHILOSOPHY OF TRANSLATION

The Philosophy of Translation

DAMION SEARLS

Yale

UNIVERSITY PRESS

New Haven & London

PUBLISHED WITH ASSISTANCE FROM THE FOUNDATION
ESTABLISHED IN MEMORY OF AMASA STONE MATHER
OF THE CLASS OF 1907, YALE COLLEGE.

Epigraph by Caitlin C. Earley, from *Lives of the Gods: Divinity in Maya Art*,
edited by Oswaldo Chinchilla Mazariegos, James A. Doyle, and Joanne
Pillsbury. Copyright © 2022 by The Metropolitan Museum of Art, New
York. Reprinted by permission.

Excerpt from "West Wall" from "Entranceway" from *The Dawning
Moon of the Mind: Unlocking the Pyramid Texts* by Susan Brind Morrow.
Copyright © 2015 by Susan Brind Morrow. Reprinted by permission of
Farrar, Straus and Giroux. All rights reserved.

Yale University Press books may be purchased in quantity for
educational, business, or promotional use. For information, please email
sales.press@yale.edu (U.S. office) or sales@yaleup.co.uk (U.K. office).

Set in Adobe Text type by Westchester Publishing Services.
Printed in the United States of America.

Library of Congress Control Number: 2024939088
ISBN 978-0-300-24737-4 (hardcover : alk. paper)

A catalogue record for this book is available from the British Library.

This paper meets the requirements of ANSI/NISO Z39.48-1992
(Permanence of Paper).

10 9 8 7 6 5 4 3 2 1

"Impersonation" is an imperfect translation of the Maya term *ubaa-hil aan/ahn* (it is his/her image), written using a hieroglyph of a pocket gopher with the glyph *k'an* (precious/yellow) infixed in its cheek. When ritually impersonating a god, a ruler assumed part of the deity's vital essence—a layering, rather than a replacement, of identities. . . . Viewers would have understood both identities to be present, the vital power of universal gods infusing the actions of the ruler.

—CAITLIN C. EARLEY,
  Lives of the Gods: Divinity in Maya Art

CONTENTS

INTRODUCTION

Reading like a Translator

In my late twenties, when I was interested in maybe becoming a translator but didn't know how to go about doing such a thing, my mother suggested I try getting in touch with our old neighborhood friend Edie. I had read Dr. Seuss at her apartment on the Upper West Side of Manhattan, later babysat her son. She's stopped teaching and become a translator, my mother said. What language? I asked. My mother didn't know, maybe Spanish?

Wait a minute, Edie Grossman was Edith Grossman, legendary translator of García Márquez and soon to be of Cervantes?

I got back in touch, and Edie kindly agreed to let me send her my first translation effort, a short descriptive vignette by Peter Handke. She knew no German, had never read Handke, but took a look. Along with being encouraging about my translation and nicer than it deserved, she gave

1

me some advice: Don't use "-ing" words if you can help it, she said, they're weak in English. Don't say there's a *gleaming* in the snow, say there's a *gleam*; instead of a cocoon *hanging* in the trees, say it *hung* in the trees. She circled three of the "-ing" words in my translation and said that those were all right but I should recast the rest. When I looked back at the German, those three—only those three—had the "-d" verb suffix analogous to "-ing." The verb I had translated "was hanging" could be "hung"; the noun could be a gleam, not a gleaming.

In telling this story over the years, I've found that other translators tend to be less impressed by it than nontranslators. But at the time I was one of those nontranslators, and it gave me an eerie sense of being in the presence of greatness: Grossman knew what she was doing, Handke knew what he was doing, and they could commune with each other right through me. Aside from the practical lesson—not a single one of the, I don't know, a million? verbs I have run across in the twenty-five years since then have I translated without thinking about this advice—the encounter taught me something else too: that translation didn't work the way I thought. Edie knew no German at all, and even if her advice was the product of her expertise in English, her matching the exact three and only three participles in German was a feat of reading, not just of good English-language writing. It was not a matter of linguistic competence, or not only, and while clearly it involved mastery in something to do with language, it was not any kind of mastery I understood. Whatever the process is that transforms an original into a translation, she was doing it, and if I ever wanted to do it too I was not going to learn how simply by improving my German.

It is indisputable, I think, that translation is a certain kind of writing linked to or coordinated with a certain kind of reading. This isn't a definition of translation yet, because we haven't said *what kind* of reading and writing they are and how they go together, but I think it's undeniably true as far as it goes: translating is reading one text and writing another where there's some specific relationship between the two.

In this combination, I would argue that writing as a translator is pretty much the same as any other kind of writing. A translator uses the resources of the language they're writing in to produce a text that will be read and received within the context of that language. A translation into English is going to find its place in a literary universe—and a literary marketplace—of other *English* texts, so a translator of, say, Chinese poetry has to find a version of *English* poetry in which the poems will make sense to their readers. The translator can't do what writers in Chinese do—can't lean on the resources of the Chinese language, can't try to do what the original text is doing in the original language—they have to make a text that does something worthwhile in English.

This is another way to say that a translator is not just a copyist, trying to replicate the original as closely as possible: a translator is necessarily producing new work in and for a new context—in this case an English-language context—different from the original's. One key fact about that new context, for instance, is whether or not the author is already a known quantity there; if they are, you have to think about what you want your intervention to be: are you trying to just add more work to the author's existing corpus in English, or to redefine the author, emphasizing aspects of their work you think have been underappreciated? Your goal will sometimes push you to translate more closely, if you feel something has been missing in English, and sometimes more freely, if you feel the ground has been covered well and you can take the basics for granted. There are wider aspects of the context as well: whatever the status of the specific author, translators are often trying to change the new audience's more fundamental expectations of what's possible. (I sometimes want to show English-language readers that German writing *can* be funny; the translator Anton Hur wants to show English-language readers that there *are* contemporary queer voices in Korean; Daisy Rockwell, a translator from Hindi, wants to show that there *are* timeless, world-class, "canonical" novels in hitherto underrepresented languages . . .) These aspirations will affect what you decide to translate, how you make the books sound, and how you publicize and talk about them.

As writers go, a translator operates under an especially strong constraint: to produce a text that's a translation of the original, not some random new thing. But every writer operates under constraints, of genre and tradition and readerly expectations and the language itself. Even if you're writing your very own novel, you still have to do what a novel is supposed to do in English in 2024 in the United States or wherever you are, in the realist tradition or some anti-realist tradition, or else you have to recognizably push against those expectations. That is how you and everybody else will know that what you're writing is a novel in English, as opposed to something else. So that's a difference in degree from the constraints on producing a translation, not a difference in kind. Translation *is* unlike other cases because it involves another language, but there are some kinds of analysis where this particular difference makes a difference and others where it doesn't. For example, when you're talking about a translation as being a take on, or version of, the original—like a performer's specific way of interpreting a preexisting piece of music—then the fact that the translation is in a different language is more of a technicality.

But while writing as a translator is pretty much the same as writing like anyone else, reading as a translator is different from just reading. The defining feature of the act of translation is the kind of reading the translator is doing, and the philosophical account of translation in this book is of what it means to read like a translator. This book is not a craft book of tips on how to write translations, unless it counts as a tip to encourage translators to pay attention to as much of what you care about as you possibly can. In other words: read as deeply and completely as possible, and read like a translator in the ways I will describe, while practicing the same art and craft of writing as in nontranslated texts.

I will begin with, but quickly abandon, the nearly universal and often unexamined image of translation as bringing an original text from one language into another. This is an image of two isolated villages or islands, separated by some kind of gap, with no contact between them except that lone, special, unusually mobile person, the translator, who is able to bring messages from one place to the other, maybe even occasionally smuggle in some food. Although this is sometimes the right way to talk about translation, it usually isn't. It creates all sorts of false dichotomies, mischaracterizes what translators actually do, misrepresents the continuities between translation and other kinds of writing, and misunderstands the nature of reading.

Reading—"this fruitful miracle of communication in the bosom of solitude," as Proust called it in a translator's preface— is miraculously and mysteriously neither objective nor subjective, neither purely taking something in nor purely revealing or expressing what's inside oneself. It is a complex interplay of the self and the world, analogous to perception—we see what's really there in the world, but *we* see it, and it's there in *our* world, the environment we move in and care about, which is different from the environment of any other person or animal in the same physical space. Likewise, we read the book itself, but *we* read it, from *our* particular perspective. And when we translate the book, we translate our reading of the original. A view of translation as first and foremost *reading* has surprisingly wide-ranging consequences, from what it means to translate "faithfully" to the abilities of ChatGPT.

One reason to call this process "reading"—as opposed to calling it "analyzing" or "understanding" the original—is the different amount or kind of authority it presupposes. As a translator I feel that I read deeply and well, but not that my reading outranks or preempts other readings, the way a correct interpretation or analysis implicitly criticizes incorrect ones. I can and do sometimes criticize other translations as wrong, or bad, but this process feels entirely separate and detached from the translation process: it feels as if once we have rejected a mistranslation, we are no step closer to arriving at our own preferred translation. I want to describe translation as something like moving through the world, not anything like choosing from a list of options.

Happily, it is now possible to take for granted that translation is not just the poor stepchild of literary production—a mechanical, work-for-hire job in more or less the same category as typesetting—but a rich and fascinating practice that sheds light on many facets of art and the human condition. This has not always been the case, but in the past ten or fifteen years several prominent translators, including Edith Grossman in her 2010 book *Why Translation Matters*, have published personal records or reminiscences with an advocacy component—translation really is important, creative, vital—that the author proves by example. Two other recent general-audience books in English have been written by translators to introduce readers who may not have thought seriously about translation to the interesting issues involved: David Bellos's *Is That a Fish in Your Ear?* (2011) and Mark Polizzotti's *Sympathy for the Traitor* (2018). In addition, the past forty or fifty years have seen an explosion of academic studies of translation, creating an institutional position for work that often, unfortunately, remains divorced from real practice, unusable and in some cases nearly unreadable by most of the people who actually produce translations. Now is a good time for a more general study of the nature and meaning of translation, tied more closely to the real experience of translating, not written in an academic voice for a purely academic audience, not needing to argue the value of the enterprise from scratch, and aiming to make a contribution to the theory and practice of the art rather than offer an introduction to it.

George Steiner's *After Babel: Aspects of Language and Translation* (1975) magisterially framed the entire human and cultural condition as a process of interpreting and recasting—in short, translation. Written before the rise of translation studies as an academic field, it was freer to roam across time and space than books from our more specialized era. The present book does not try to speak from Steiner's mandarin, Olympian position decreeing everything from on high, but it does set out to make an argument about what translation is and how it works, how it feels, challenging and correcting some reigning ideas about translation.

I hope to somewhat sidestep the domain of "translation theory," although I remain optimistic that the book will be of interest and use to people studying or writing translation theory. What is "theory"? Steiner gets very worked up in *After Babel* about people claiming to offer any translation theory at all, by which he means any "'theoretic' meaning susceptible of inductive generalization, prediction, and falsifiability of counter-example." No such science of translation is possible, Steiner argues—no "systematic model of the general structure and epistemological validity of the transfer of meaning between languages."[1] Clearly, this hard-science model of experiment and falsifiable hypotheses is not what the theory-people mean by "theory," although I am not going to try to nail down a definition of theory here, nor a hard and fast distinction between theory and philosophy.

I will say that theory naturally creates tension with practice and practitioners: while definitionally opposed to practice, theory also leans in toward it, always more or less suggesting the foolishness or impossibility of trying to engage in the practice without applying the theory. "You can't do this thing without an implicit or explicit theory behind your actions," say the theorists, but lots of practitioners don't read or care about theory and don't want to be told they have an "implicit" one in their head that some theorist knows more about than they do. In my experience, most or at least many practicing translators find translation theory irrelevant at best, importunate at worst—much as the high points of high theory back in the day, "deconstruction" or "the death of the author," had little to offer most practicing novelists. Polizzotti's self-proclaimed Translation Manifesto calls most translation theory "flashy," "prescriptive," "prohibitive," "plainly abstruse," and "not of much use when it comes to looking at what translation is—or . . . *does*,"

1. George Steiner, *After Babel: Aspects of Language and Translation* (Oxford University Press, 1975; 3rd ed., 1998), pp. 287–290.

saying about his own book: "Consider this rather an 'antitheory,' or perhaps just a common-sense approach."[2] I don't claim to be writing antitheory, or speaking for good old solid common sense, but I am trying to describe what translators do rather than define or mandate what they should or must do. I don't aspire to have my ideas "applied" by practicing translators, but I do hope they find these ideas suggestive, illuminating, or at least lovely.

Another difference I see between theory and philosophy is that a work of theory necessarily positions itself with and against the other theories out there, and the more the better; in writing theory you spend a lot of time citing other theorists just to say how you agree or disagree with them. Part of my understanding of this book as philosophy instead means that I intend it as a primary text, not a secondary text about other approaches. Comprehensive coverage of all the theories out there, mastery of the field, has never been my strong suit, and in any case I wanted to write this book for the uninitiated as well. I sometimes make use of earlier works of philosophy or the history of ideas so as not to have to reinvent the wheel, and I cite other translators' experiences in an effort to base my philosophy on more than just my personal background, but I am not concerned to position my views "in the field," and I try my best to refrain from name-checking other theorists or philosophers simply to show that I've read them. Most of

2. Mark Polizzotti, *Sympathy for the Traitor: A Translation Manifesto* (MIT Press, 2018), p. xiii.

what I say, probably all of what I say, has been said before by other people, some of whom I have read, more of whom have been pointed out to me in early responses to my manuscript, and still more of whom will continue to come my way in the future—but I am not trying to give the impression that what I think is true is also original.

A book calling itself *The Philosophy of Translation* seems to claim to offer a universal, or at least generally applicable, account of what translation is, but any philosopher nowadays knows two things: First, that their own frame of reference is provincial. I am writing in a basically French, English, German, and Russian tradition based on Latin and Greek; I am not familiar enough with, for instance, Chinese, Indian, Arabic, African, and Native American traditions of translation, or even philosophies from modern Western European nations not listed here, for any genuine claim to universality to be anything but laughable. Second, that not everyone even in the philosopher's own provincial audience will agree with them. While every philosophy seen from within, so to speak, is "*The* Philosophy of X" (of translation, of law, of nature . . .), when seen from the outside it is "*A* Philosophy of X" among all the many others, an artifact as partial and debatable as any. I often think of the Borges line that metaphysics should be considered a subgenre of speculative fiction—an act of "world creation," as the sci-fi writers say. Different philosophies are like different alternate universes. And yet I offer my take on translation from within, as what I really believe—*The* Philosophy of Translation.

This stance, offering readers *the* philosophy of something, feels to me not like imperious arrogance but rather as a kind of humility. It is not claiming to speak for everybody; it is defining a position with as little hedging as possible and offering it to readers so that they can decide what they think of it, leaving them fully free to take it or leave it. The philosopher asks to be believed not from without but from within: not "See and understand my experience, which has authority over yours," but "Reflect on your own experience and test my claims against it." Philosophy portrays something about the world but doesn't introduce this thing as an empirical fact or prove it scientifically; it offers reminders or reconsiderations, redirections, little stories (Plato's about Socrates's conversations, Wittgenstein's about playing games) meant to solicit our agreement. Underlying this solicitation is a certain conception of community and shared human nature.

As with translation, we want to walk the line—not an especially fine line, but not infinitely wide either—between believing that another person or culture is forever alien, exotic, and impenetrable to us (everyone's experience is irreconcilably different) and believing that there is no problem with speaking in our language for these others (my personal truth is Philosophy Itself); in other words, between the narcissistic belief that no one else has anything to say to us and the equally narcissistic belief that it's never a problem to recast what other people say in our own voice. Translation always admits, and revels in, the differences between languages, versions, cultures, and people, and at the same time always claims, and aims at, a common language able not just to "bridge" but to actually remove these divides. Indeed, the same dynamic will reappear again and again in this book: the argument that once you posit a fundamental gap, you won't be able to bridge it. One thing I hope my book's title does is own up to the fact that I lean toward believing divides can be crossed and ideas are applicable in more than one context.

This book falls into two halves, with the first four chapters providing a history of ideas of translation and most of the philosophical argument, while the last four chapters contain most of the concrete translation examples and a coda. The examples are taken primarily from my own work, not because my translation decisions are better than everybody else's but because I have inside knowledge about them; my goal is not to pat myself on the back (except for the decision about the dog's name—I'm proud of that one), but to connect these decisions or practices to the philosophical terms I'm laying out.

In fact, one thing that makes translation such an intellectually rich topic is how amenable it is to examples. It's so obvious what a translation is: you don't need an argument to explain it. When I was teaching expository writing to first-year students at a highly selective college, I found that in general they didn't arrive knowing the difference between an opinion and an argument, so they didn't understand how I could grade their papers, at least with anything less than another "A" like they were used to. How can you give my paper a "C," they implicitly or explicitly cried, I'm entitled to my opinion! The math and science majors in particular tended to imagine that I, the teacher, had a secret checklist of what made an essay or argument "right" and their job was to guess it, because, after all, in their disciplines what makes something a problem is that it has right and wrong answers. These difficulties solved themselves, one might say, when I organized the course around the topic of translation. It was self-evidently clear to my students that there are better and worse translations even though there's no single right one: a translation can be more or less accurate, elegant, perceptive, persuasive, justified, revelatory, beautiful. So too—the analogy drew itself—their paper, their analysis of *The Great Gatsby* or a Shakespeare sonnet, could be better or worse without being right or wrong.

There would have been advantages to alternating chapters of philosophy and example in this book, or otherwise interspersing the two, but I found that keeping them mostly separate made it easier to follow the argument. One of the (I hope) appeals of this book, but also one of its (I admit) challenges, is that it brings together arguments and ideas from disciplines and reading lists that are usually quite distinct, clustered around an idiosyncratic core of thinkers not generally read in the context of translation: Maurice Merleau-Ponty, Viktor Shklovsky, Mikhail Bakhtin. Almost all readers will find some topics in chapters 1–4 that are new and unfamiliar to them, as well as summaries of well-known topics that are annoyingly basic but are meant for people with differing areas of expertise. For instance, my introduction to "phenomenology" will be well-trodden ground for anyone steeped in philosophy, and

I hope these readers will forgive its rehashing of the obvious, but it is intended for the benefit of those without that background; vice versa for my definitions of "source language" and "target language." I imagine there are readers of this book who will prefer to skip the philosophy altogether in favor of the examples, or to read chapters 5–7 and then chapters 1–4. But a book has to start somewhere.

THE HISTORY OF "TRANSLATION"

A good place to start is with the word "translation" itself. *Trans-latio*, from the Latin for "to carry across," suggests that translators "bring" an original text across "a gap" "from" "somewhere else." What else could translation be?

In the standard way of discussing translation, these two places—the starting point and end point of this process of transportation—are the "source language" and the "target language." For *War and Peace*, the source language is Russian and the target language is English; for *La guerre et la paix* the source is Russian and the target is French. I personally prefer the term "translating language" to "target language," to avoid the violent archery or artillery image and because a target is too passive—*War and Peace* wasn't shot at English, it was written *in* English—but "target" is far more common. Both labels can be specified further, for instance by saying the source language is aristocratic nineteenth-century Russian from Tolstoy's particular region; an earlier translation's target language might be nineteenth-century British English and you might want a translation into twenty-first-century American English. In any case, there is a thing that exists in one place, and the translator brings it, keeping it as intact as possible, to another place. After this process, the same thing now exists in two places: readers can read Tolstoy's novel, the same book, in English or Russian.

The source/target terminology is surprisingly recent, but the framework is usually traced back to an 1813 lecture, "On the Different Methods of Translating," by the German theologian and philosopher Friedrich Schleiermacher.[1] For Schleiermacher, there are two "Different Methods of Translating," and only two, because the translator is someone who "wants to bring two completely separated persons truly together: his author and his reader," letting the reader "understand and enjoy" the author "as correctly and completely as possible without forcing the reader out of the sphere of his mother tongue." That means "either the translator leaves the author in peace, as much as possible, and moves the reader toward him; or he leaves the reader in peace, as much as possible, and moves the author toward him." Summaries of Schleiermacher often stop there.

1. Schleiermacher's German original, "Ueber der verschiedenen Methoden des Uebersezens," is easily available online; the most readily available English translation is Susan Bernofsky's, in *The Translation Studies Reader*, 3rd ed., ed. Lawrence Venuti (Routledge, 2012), pp. 43–63. Translations here are mine.

These options also tend to be equated, or reduced, to a different dichotomy: on the one hand there is "domesticating" translation, making the text seem as natural as possible to the target audience, and on the other hand there is "foreignizing" translation, which leaves the text more or less alien and makes the reader do more work. When you're translating a novel, you can either leave the money in a foreign currency and expect the reader to know or go look up how much a thousand francs or a string of coins is worth, or you can convert the amount into dollars. You can call them gauchos, or decide that it's close enough if you call them cowboys. You can use a foreign word for the culturally specific food we don't have here, or you can paraphrase and explain it as "vegetable paste" or "spicy bean porridge" or whatever it is. The latter is neither as accurate nor as specific—you won't get to a real mental image of goulash from reading "paprika meat soup," and nobody in the world would actually want to eat something called "vegetable paste" (but eba is delicious!)—still, if you translate like this you are leaving readers in peace as much as possible, not intimidating them with any foreign words, and sacrificing some of the foreign reality as needed. The decision to domesticate or foreignize also extends far beyond terminology and word choice, to genre, storytelling conventions, plot structure, poetic form, visions of human (or for that matter nonhuman) character, and anything else about a text that may feel more natural in the original context than in the context of the translation. An American translator can adapt the text to American readers' purported expectations or can leave it more or less alien, either out of loyalty to the cultural specificity of the original or out of a sense that the reader could use a little more educational exposure to a different culture's realities.

Naturally, a translator can also do both, especially in the narrow case of unfamiliar words or terms ("a string of coins, roughly a week's wages"; "eba made from the local cassavas"), but the polarity between domesticating and foreignizing remains, and organizes many current discussions of translation. Theorists often pick a side and valorize either the source or the target. Editors and publishers have their preferences too: in the English-speaking world, they have long tended to want domesticating translations, to make things easier on the mass readership they're hoping for and also because reviewers tend to praise a translation that's "seamless" and "transparent," something that doesn't seem like a translation, although on the other hand with just the right amount of easily understood local color. Especially since the 1990s, academic theorists of translation have tended to go in the other direction from these commercial publishers, valorizing the foreign and opposing the ethnocentric erasure of difference by dominant, hegemonic English.

The dichotomy is almost always grounded in Schleiermacher's essay, as I too have done here, so it's somewhat shocking to learn that the essay itself was first published in English only in 1977, in an anthology published in the Netherlands and translated by a Belgian academic.[2] It was Lawrence Venuti, an American translator from Italian, French, and Catalan and a pioneer of this branch of translation theory, who brought Schleiermacher and domestication/foreignization to prominence. In *The Translator's Invisibility* (1995), Venuti explicitly says that "violence resides in the very purpose and activity of translation" because translation is a "forcible replacement of the linguistic and cultural differences" with "values, beliefs and representations that preexist it in the target language, always configured in hierarchies of dominance and marginality." He goes on that "the violence wreaked by translation is partly inevitable, inherent in the translation process, [and] partly potential," depending on the situation, and he calls for translators to adopt a foreignizing approach that limits or undoes the damage as much as possible. After quoting the same Schleiermacher passage I just did, Venuti frames the two options as "an ethnocentric reduction of the foreign text to target-language cultural values" or "an ethnodeviant pressure on those values to register the linguistic and cultural difference of the foreign text."[3] And if the choice is between ethnocentric reduction and registering multiculturalism, you know which team he's going to be on.

Many debates in especially Anglo-American translation studies were then locked into this framework, revolving

2. Lawrence Venuti, *The Translator's Invisibility: A History of Translation* (Routledge, 1995), p. 98; the anthology is André Lefevere, ed. and tr., *Translating Literature: The German Tradition from Luther to Rosenzweig* (Van Gorcum, 1977).
3. *Translator's Invisibility*, chapter 1, "Invisibility," pp. 3–34.

around whether translation is always violent as Venuti describes; the ways in which it's collaborative, or a service to
the source text rather than an erasure of it; how this dynamic
of "forcible replacement" plays out in language pairs with different power relations between them (as in translations out of
English, or from one less-dominant language into another).
But all these debates rested, tacitly or explicitly, on the idea
of a source language over there and a target culture over here,
with the translator deciding to privilege one or the other.

And the more you look at it, as more recent translation
theorists have been doing too, the more incoherent the
distinction between "foreignizing" and "domesticating"
translations starts to seem. What is a "foreignizing" translation anyway? As Venuti says outright, no translation is truly
foreign, because any translation into English is written in
English, any translation into Chinese is written in Chinese.
A bad guy in a World War II movie saying "Vee haff vays uff
makink you tock" isn't speaking German, he is speaking a
form of English that connotes Germanness in English (this
example is mine, not Venuti's). Ezra Pound's translation of the
Anglo-Saxon poem "The Seafarer"—the classic example of a
"foreignizing" translation, since it exudes a very alien, archaic
vibe—doesn't use Anglo-Saxon: it uses various resources of
English from Pound's day to give a foreign or archaic impression, and Venuti lists them: Middle English usages like *aye* for
"always"; Victorian archaisms that had become poetic, such as
bide, *brine*, *o'er*, and *laud*; neologisms evoking Anglo-Saxon
alliteration, like "bitter breast-cares." Nor, for that matter, did

Anglo-Saxon sound archaic to the original Anglo-Saxon audience. Pound was a modern poet writing in English to readers of modern English poetry, in a complex relation to the foreign text and to all the traditions spanning the gap between it and modern English.

Another example Venuti gives is of the early standard translations of Freud into English. These, as Venuti discusses well, make Freud much more scientific sounding, intellectual, and impersonal than he is in the German original. Freud's German words which were translated as the clinical-sounding "ego" and "id" are closer to "self" and "thing," or "the I" and "the It"; "libido" could have been translated with equal accuracy as simply "sex drive"; slips of the tongue, forgetting names, losing umbrellas, and so on get called "parapraxes" in the standard translations, even though they're just "screw-ups" of various kinds.

Freud's translators strove to sound sciency for several reasons, including the disciplinary alignment of psychoanalysis with medicine and the dominance of positivist, behaviorist, quantifiable approaches in Anglo-American thought as a whole. The translators, in other words, "domesticated" Freud's writing for the Anglo-American readers they wanted, and then a positivistic reading of Freud became entrenched in Anglo-American psychoanalysis, so the translations seemed fine. Another strategy would have been to take what Venuti calls the "foreignizing" approach and read against the grain for discontinuities and other registers in the original.

All this is perfectly admirable, and Venuti analyzes the strengths and weaknesses of these translations sharply, but there's no reason to call the good approach "foreignizing." He just labels sensitivity to the original as foreignizing, and blindness or insensitivity to various registers as domesticating, because he's in the grip of a metaphor where there are only two poles, and one of them's bad, one of them's good. He even says that analyses such as his of the Freud translations "can be said to foreignize a domesticating translation by showing where it is discontinuous"—in other words, we can turn a "domesticating" translation into a "foreignizing" one just by looking at it properly! In a new 2018 introduction to *The Translator's Invisibility*, Venuti explicitly acknowledges that "all translation . . . , including translation that seeks to register linguistic and cultural differences, is an interpretation that fundamentally domesticates the source text" (as I put it, registering difference isn't "foreignizing"; both good and bad translations are "domesticating"). And at one point he suddenly gives a third option: there's domesticating, foreignizing, and *exoticizing* translation, the last of which basically means foreignizing in a bad way. So it turns out foreignizing can be ethnocentric too.[4]

Really, these are all value judgments (ethnocentric or sensitive) disguised as a conceptual difference (domesticating or foreignizing). There are ways to judge a translation—whether

4. *Translator's Invisibility*, 3rd ed. (Routledge, 2018), pp. viii–xix.

it is respectful or disrespectful, accurate or inaccurate, readable or unreadable. (Incidentally, these three standards are Plato's: as Socrates reminds Euthyphro, the three kinds of disagreement that cause contention and strife are those over what is just and unjust, good and bad, beautiful and ugly.) But the categories of "foreignizing" and "domesticating" obscure these standards rather than illuminating them. What Venuti calls "foreignizing" translation is probably closest to the criterion of being "respectful" to the original, but misleadingly put.

One explanation for why we have ended up with such incoherent ideas about translation, and with these ideas in particular, lies in their history, and reviewing how we got here can help us understand, if not quite disentangle, the competing and contradictory strands in how we think about translation today. In the so-called Western tradition this book is operating in—basically Greek-Latin-French-English-German-Russian— there have been two important reconceptualizations of what translation is, and one later reconceptualization of the nature of language which had important consequences for translation. None of these new understandings of translation fully refuted or replaced the previous one, leaving us with ideas about translation from various frameworks that are in tension or outright contradiction with one another.

Antoine Berman tracks the first two of these redefinitions in an important essay that has not been translated from French into English, full of information that I have not seen anywhere else, so I will quote and summarize his essay at greater length than I do the other secondary sources I discuss in this book.[5] He traces the Latinate roots of "translation"—in French the word is *"traduction"*—back to classical Roman culture; at this starting point, there was no specific word for the activity we call translation. Cicero used the words *vertere* (turn), *convertere* (convert), *verbum pro verbo reddere* (render word for word), and more to describe this process, while *"translatio"* in classical Latin meant the physical transport of objects or people, the handing over of rights or jurisdiction, or in short what we would call "transfer."

The organizing principle in the Roman context was not so much language as *traditio*: a linking with the past, reasserting for the present, and carrying forward into the future. An *auctor* was not today's creative "author" but an "augmenter" or "aggrandizer"; insofar as the translation of Greek texts into Latin was a transfer or *translatio*, it was a transfer of authority that added something. The Greeks were cast as an "authority" to the Romans (which is not what they were originally to their fellow Greeks); the Latin world annexed the Greek; and authority was thereby "transferred" to the Romans (in scare quotes because this authority didn't actually exist as such in Greece before the Romans retroactively defined it as what

5. Antoine Berman, "Tradition, Translation, Traduction," *Le cahier* 6 (1988): 21–38; translations below are mine. Another discussion of Berman's essay at some length in English is in Katharina N. Piechocki, "Cartographic Translation: Reframing Leonardo Bruni's *De interpretatione recta* (1424)," *I Tatti Studies in the Italian Renaissance* 20.1 (Spring 2017): 41–65, a fascinating argument linking modern translation theory to the spatial conceptions of modern cartography.

they were taking over). Tradition is anchored to a particular place of origin—a Greek text has authority fundamentally unlike that of a text in some other language—although the fact that a tradition can grow and move proves the existence of an underlying common humanity.

In the fourteenth century, along with the transfer or geographical displacement of imperial power (*translatio imperii*) came a new understanding of the transfer of knowledge (*translatio studii*). Knowledge exists to be transferred—that is its destiny, that is what defines it as knowledge: it is invariant content, independent of a particular language and place of origin, and *translatio* is the process of moving that content, specifically into vernacular languages and their countries. This is the first major redefinition, from augmentative "transfer" to something more like "translation." Along with translation, we also have for the first time "communication": it was Nicolas Oresme (c. 1323–1382), the theoretician of *translatio studii*, translator of Aristotle, and counselor to King Charles V of France, who introduced the new word "*communication*" into French. Latin, as Berman puts it, was *not* a language of communication, like French in the seventeenth century or English today, but instead a language of "communion": shared, sacred, inherently linked to the Christian tradition. Translation, in contrast, is communication, circulation, the ungrounded transfer of what is transferable. And what is transferable is all that matters. Finally, translation in this mode is still inherently augmentative, but in new ways. In the Middle Ages, the augmentation took the form of additions to make the text clearer;

providing glosses; and restructuring the original under head-
ings, subheadings, and other indications of order. In the modern age, we have footnotes, putting words in italics, adding
introductions and afterwords—all designed to transfer knowledge more effectively.

Berman lists three particular corollaries or consequences
of this new understanding, the *translatio* model. (1) Translation as communication requires *clarity*: the ideal goal is now a
"clear and distinct" transfer of the language-transcending content. In fact, historically, the ideal of clarity was *first* a requirement for translation, only later for writing itself. (2) Since
thought is taken to be independent of the contingent and tran-
sitory vessel of its language, there is no problem with translations of translations. It was perfectly legitimate for Oresme to
translate Aristotle from Latin, not Greek. (3) The translation
of ungrounded, transportable content is indifferent to tradition, rejecting any unique sacred origin and any traditional
bond (*religio*) to that origin. Most notably, Bible translations
into vernacular languages, eventually culminating in the critical philology of the nineteenth century, traduce the Holy
Book, betraying and profaning it, turning communion into
mere communication. Whereas a tradition is always a specific
tradition, in modernity "all that is solid melts into air"—a loss
of both specific traditions and, more painfully, groundedness
or traditionality as such. This is why Bibles in vernacular languages were so threatening.

In the Renaissance, this practice of translation continued, while being reconceptualized again and for the first

time given its own name: *traductio*, or in its French form *traduction*. This is the second major shift. Leonardo Bruni, an Italian humanist and the author of a 1424 treatise on correct or straight interpretation (*De interpretatione recta*), introduced the term *traductio* for translation,[6] and within roughly a century, *traducere* and *traductio* became the words for translation throughout Latinate Europe (French *traduire/ traduction*, Spanish *traducir/traducción*, Italian *tradurre/ traduzione*)—except in English, which kept the earlier Latinate *translate/translation*.[7]

While *translatio* was understood as the clear and distinct transfer of *content*—language-independent knowledge— *traductio* was taken to mean finding and relaying the *form* of

6. Famously, Bruni's use of this word is said to have been based on a mistranslation! In the original work by the Roman grammarian Aulus Gellius that Bruni referred to, it meant a "borrowing" of a Greek word in Latin, not a translation. George Steiner calls this misinterpretation "trivial but symbolic. Often, in the records of translation, a fortunate misreading is the source of new life" (*After Babel*, p. 311). But see Piechocki, "Cartographic Translation," 59–61, for a more extended and nuanced discussion of Bruni's Roman and Scholastic sources.

7. Why is English different? Berman, writing in French, mentions the English exception but has no reason to discuss it further. I am not aware of any research on why the word "traduction" never took hold in English, and whether the divergence means anything about different cultures of translation, but it would be a fascinating subject. Do the supposedly more commonsensical English have a more goal-oriented vision of *translatio* as knowledge-transfer rather than the more aesthetic and mystical *traductio*, for instance? Did keeping the older terminology contribute to making the conceptual jumble about translation worse in English? The *Oxford English Dictionary* gives a few sixteenth-century examples of "traduce" and "traduction" in the sense of translation, along with some more or less arch and ironic later uses, so it was a linguistic option in the culture, a possible path not taken.

the work. The form of a work (which also had content) was analogous to the soul of a person (who also had a body). To recap: originally, what was carried over was *authority* (e.g., Greek authority into the Latin world); in the pre-Renaissance model, *content* was brought into a new vernacular language; now the object of translation was *the work*, with its indissoluble fusion of content and form, body and soul, and translation became the task of preserving the soul or essence of the original in an entirely new body.

Here, in this conceptualization, we have the birth of the notion that translation is "impossible." During the development of vernacular languages, translation was, so to speak, contingently impossible—impossible for now—but someday, once a modern language improved enough, through word borrowings, neologisms, and the development of more advanced rhetorical techniques, it would be able convey the "eloquence" of the classical original as well as its content.[8] Content and eloquence were seen as separable, with the latter harder to translate but eventually possible. In the newer framework of *traductio*, in contrast, content and form are inseparable and translation is thus intrinsically paradoxical. If a work's essence is its fusion of soul and body, ideas and words, there simply cannot be the same fusion when all the words are different. Similarly new is the insistence that the most important thing

8. R. F. Jones, *The Triumph of the English Language* (Stanford University Press, 1951), entertainingly reviews the contemporary debates about how best to improve the inadequate language of pre-Elizabethan English.

is "lost in translation": before *traductio*, translation was assumed to be quite a large net gain.

No longer a mere movement or transfer of anything, translation-as-*traduction* is now a transformative energy, the work of an active subject.[9] No longer merely more or less clear, it is now *imitative* and *innovative*: an attempt to truly reproduce the original, in effect to produce a new original. Ideally, translations in this model are eloquent, even seductive. The goal is not clarity but beauty. Translation starts to be seen as a training ground for writers (medieval translations, Berman remarks, are often much more poorly written than their dedications; *translateurs* did not try to "mobilize all the resources of the language" as they did in their original writing, but *traducteurs* do). And once the original is understood as a special work with a unique soul, translations of translations are rejected as self-evidently illegitimate because they are two steps removed from that original instead of just one, which is bad enough.

The shift from a *translatio* model to a *traductio* model was far from complete, and ever since, "translation" has been a jumble of these different concepts. "We exist today," Berman writes, "in the age of universal *translation* proclaimed by Nicolas Oresme, but also in the age of the *traduction* of forms proclaimed by

9. Berman, building on Michel Serres, classifies "*traduction*" within the family of -*duction* words, which have to do with transformative, generative, creative energy: *production, reproduction, reduction, deduction, induction, seduction, introduction*. See Piechocki, "Cartographic Translation," p. 48, for the Serres references, with quotations.

Bruni. As a result, every translator finds themselves subject to a double law. Are they *translateur* or *traducteur*?" Saying we are "subject to a double law" is snappy, and very French, but it has little explanatory power and there are real contradictions between the two models. With *translatio*, translation is always possible (knowledge exists to be transferred); with *traductio*, translation is never possible (form and content are fused in the original). The idea that something is always "lost in translation" exists in the *traductio* framework, while ideas of expanding our horizons, "building bridges between cultures," and so forth are in the *translatio* framework. In practice, translators are always switching back and forth between these models, while many of the endless old translation debates—beautiful or accurate? form or content? possible or impossible?—should really be seen as pointless cross talk between the two. Arguments about whether secondhand or "relay" translations are legitimate or illegitimate, for instance, often consist of the two sides simply talking past each other.[10]

10. Here is an example of how the debate tends to look: Rita Chowdhury, an Assam poet, recently argued that for Assamese-to-English translations it is "better" to "go through a 'via language' process. For example, if we translate an Assamese book into Hindi first then it becomes easier to get quality translation work from Hindi into English because there are lots of quality Hindi-language translators who have good command over both Hindi and English. The problem with most Assamese translators is that if one has a good grasp of English, he or she might not have the same grasp on the Assamese language." Michael Orthofer, in the well-known blog of the Complete Review, remarked with sarcasm or astonishment: "I don't know that I've ever heard the case made that it's *better* to translate second-hand. . . ." His *traductio*-standard of translation as preserving and re-creating the "essence" of a work is simply on a different plane than her practical *translatio*-concern with Assamese competence among writers in English.

I mentioned that after the two major reconceptualizations Berman's article describes came a third conceptual shift, not in the understanding of translation per se but rather reenvisioning what language is, with consequences for translation. This shift took place during German Romanticism, spearheaded by none other than Schleiermacher. Again it is Antoine Berman who sensitively describes the nature of this shift, but in a different book[11] than the essay I have been paraphrasing, and as far as I know he unfortunately never specifies the overlap or difference between the German Romantic shift and the *traditio-translatio-traductio* history described in his essay, except for a passing mention in the latter essay that Bruni's definition of *traductio* as a transfer of form not content marks "the birth of modern translation, and German Romanticism has nothing further to say on the subject."

Schleiermacher, along with Wilhelm von Humboldt (a translator of Xenophon and Aeschylus as well as being the

---

Rita Chowdhury, "Regional Literature Needs Quality Translators," in *Outlook India*, https://www.outlookindia.com/culture-society/regional-literature-needs-quality-translators-assamese-writer-rita-chowdhury-weekender_story-201835; Michael Orthofer, "Translation from . . . Assamese," *Literary Saloon* (blog), Complete Review, June 15, 2022, https://www.complete-review.com/saloon/archive/202206b.htm#vx6.

Personally, I feel it should be self-evident, even in the *traductio* model, that a relay translation by two excellent translators is better than a direct translation by a bad translator. To think otherwise means believing *both* that translation is always a net loss *and* that all translators are equally harmful, so two steps will necessarily take you further from the original than one step by somebody else.

11. Antoine Berman, *The Experience of the Foreign: Culture and Translation in Romantic Germany*, tr. S. Heyvaert (1984; State University of New York Press, 1992).

pioneer of modern generative linguistics),[12] redefined the relationship between people and language while linking this new
philosophy of language explicitly to translation. Both men saw
language not as a mere instrument of communication, one
among others, but as our ever-present, indispensable environment, indeed our "own being": "the ultimate medium of any
relation of man to himself, to others, and to the world." Bruni's
traductio posited an inseparability of form and content, soul
and body, within the written text, but the German Roman-
tics extended that fusion, almost mystically, into both micro-
cosm and macrocosm, arguing that the writer is profoundly
connected to, intimate with, his or her (usually his) "mother
tongue," while a language as a whole profoundly embodies the
spirit and mentality of the population or "race" that speaks
and thinks in it.[13] In Humboldt's famous formulation, language
is "not a product (*ergon*) but an activity (*energeia*)"—not an
artifact intended for some purpose, such as a tool for communication, but an involuntary emanation of one's human
nature. At the same time, languages are also "bound [to] and

12. In *On the Diversity of Human Language Construction and Its Influence on
the Mental Development of the Human Species*, published posthumously in 1836
and translated into English as *On Language* by Peter Heath, ed. and intro. Michael
Losonsky (Cambridge University Press, 1999).

13. Yasemin Yildiz, in *Beyond the Mother Tongue: The Postmonolingual Condition* (Fordham University Press, 2012), shows how the whole idea of a mother
tongue—symbolically representing "a unique, irreplaceable, unchangeable bio-
logical origin that situates the individual automatically in a kinship network and
by extension in the nation," with our relationship to this singular primary language now "emotionalized," "allegedly organic," and marked by "affective and
corporeal intimacy"—also arose in precisely this time and place (pp. 9–10).

dependent on the nations to which they belong": language is tied to how people think, and different peoples have different languages.

Schleiermacher's commitment to this framework is evident everywhere beyond and behind the few oft-quoted passages of "On the Different Methods of Translating." His lifework, to which his translation essay was a sideline, was the invention of hermeneutics as an independent discipline: a theory of intersubjective understanding as such, unlike earlier hermeneutics which focused on the proper way to understand a text in a specific field (Biblical interpretation, legal interpretation, and so on). This modern hermeneutics is necessary because, even though language is intimately fused with a person's mind, an emanation of their own being, it fails to provide pure and perfect access to that person: language is as it were opaque, not transparent, and intersubjective understanding is a task, not a given.

In Schleiermacher's translation essay in particular, this new vision of how language relates to the individual and the nation shapes much of his argument. Berman says outright that "what is interesting" in the ubiquitous Schleiermacher quote about bringing author to reader and leaving reader in peace or vice versa "is not so much the nature of the distinction (ethnocentric or nonethnocentric translation) as the manner in which it is expressed: a process of an intersubjective encounter." In other words, Schleiermacher made it personal. Once language is viewed as the inescapable vehicle and expression of the human mind, reading and translation are actions we take on other people, not just on texts. To try to produce a version of a foreign text that reads "as though the author originally wrote it in German" (or English, etc.) is to fundamentally misunderstand the intimate relationship between the original author and his or her mother tongue: according to Schleiermacher, "it is as if you brought me the man's portrait just as he would have looked if his mother had conceived him with another father." This quote is unimaginable as a classical, medieval, or Renaissance remark on translation, which shows the extent of the German Romantic innovation; despite being from Schleiermacher's same essay on translation, it is consistently absent from discussions of domesticating versus foreignizing. (Though not, of course, always absent. The third chapter of Venuti's *The Translator's Invisibility*, "Nation," contains a long and thorough discussion of these aspects of Schleiermacher; however, this chapter is rarely assigned in courses on translation theory, leaving the domestication/foreignization distinction from chapter 1 to stand on its own.)

The German Romantic vision of an intimate bond between author, language, and nation means that the task of the translator—more precisely, the task of the translating nation—is to enrich the mother tongue so that a text preserving the relationship between author and original language can be written in this tongue. For Schleiermacher, authentic translation "rests on two conditions: that the understanding of foreign works should be a thing known and desired, and that the native language itself should be capable of a certain flexibility." (In other words: conditions met by early nineteenth-century

Germany.) Here too, Schleiermacher's essay does an end run around the simplified dichotomy between foreignizing and domesticating, emphasizing the relationship to the foreign that precedes a given individual translation, as well as the fluidity and heterogeneity of the home language into which one performs the act of translation. Fundamentally, translation is not a process of doing something to one text in order to produce one other text: it is a process of educating and cultivating a whole national language community, or in Schleiermacher's words, "a transplantation of whole literatures into a language, which is meaningful and valuable only in a nation that has a definite inclination to appropriate what is foreign. Isolated works of this type are valuable only as precursors." In fact, while summaries of Schleiermacher often stop at the quote about bringing the reader to the author or bringing the author to the reader, his essay goes on to argue that only one of the two methods is valid (the first one), because really what's involved is educating and cultivating the new nation's readers. In Humboldt's words, the task of translation "is to appropriate to the language and the spirit of a nation what it does not possess, or what it possesses in a different way."[14] Current postcolonial descriptions of traditional translation practices are not very different from Humboldt's, though of course they criticize such appropriative practices rather than championing them.

14. Wilhelm von Humboldt, "Introduction to *Agamemnon*," quoted in Berman, *Experience of the Foreign*, p. 154.

This vision of language as the lifeblood of the individual and the nation doesn't especially change the concrete practice of translation, in the way that doing *traductio* looks different from doing *translatio*.[15] As I quoted Berman as saying, "German Romanticism has nothing further to say" about the Renaissance shift to modern translation practices. What the new German Romantic understanding does is raise the stakes. Now a translator is dealing not merely with a text but with the intimate core of a person, a people. Whereas, say, the practice of adding introductions and glossaries to novels translated from Arabic might once have been seen as the typical work of *translatio*, augmenting the text and transferring knowledge, now it is more likely to be seen as an exoticization and diminishment of the Egyptian or Syrian author personally and their culture as a whole, especially in contrast to translations from other languages (no one puts a glossary in the back of English-language García Márquez or Ferrante books)—an implication that the author has to be approached ethnographically and is incapable of producing true literature. A Korean-to-English translator isn't just someone who knows those two languages but someone who bears within her bilingual self the traces and legacies of neocolonial conquest and occupation; the act of translating any particular text from Korean into English intervenes in this neocolonial history. A bad translation is not

15. Berman, *Experience of the Foreign*, p. 143: "If one were to keep to the technical or ethical principles of translation [which Schleiermacher and Humboldt] express, one would be hard put to distinguish them from Goethe's or even A. W. Schlegel's. . . . Still, the perspective is different."

just clumsy or inattentive, it is ethnocentric and violent. The idea that bad translation, or translation itself, can "erase" other cultures or "appropriate" another person's voice makes sense only within the German Romantic framework.

And the victory of this framework has been decisive: at least for translations into the globally dominant English language, it now seems almost impossible to view language as a mere tool to be expanded and refined as needed. Schleiermacher erased this perspective; all his descendants in translation theory down to today see language not as a tool but as intimately coterminous with the mind and body.[16] Language is essential to personhood, and the unique bond of the "mother tongue" is correspondingly valorized. You do things "in" a language, not "with" a language. Doing something to a language is doing something to a person or culture.

At the same time, it is hard to reconcile the sweeping, majestic claims for translation as critical to the national interest, made by Schleiermacher or Humboldt, with the relatively marginal status of literary translation in the English

16. Yildiz (see note 13 above) in fact demonstrates that Schleiermacher formulated the modern idea of the mother tongue by contrasting it to the view of language as an external, interchangeable tool: she quotes (pp. 8–9) the passage in his essay on translation where he argues that "no one adheres to his language only mechanically, as if it were something externally attached to him like a strap and as if one could as easily harness another language for one's thought as one would exchange a team of horses; rather, every writer can produce original work only in his mother tongue, and therefore the question cannot even be raised how he would have written his works in another language."

language today, in book reviews, in the funding of foreign-language departments. Even as English-language book buyers seem increasingly interested in translated literature, the fact that these books are translated has become less important: they're just good books, and who cares that Elena Ferrante originally wrote them in Italian.[17] Rarely if ever is a translation hailed the way German translations of Plato or Sophocles or Shakespeare were in the Romantic era: as vital works of nation building. Even when a canonical book from the past is retranslated and Grossman's Cervantes or Pevear and Volokhonsky's Dostoyevsky or Lydia Davis's Flaubert is celebrated, the celebration remains in the merely aesthetic realm.

The lingering influence of all these different ideas makes it difficult to explain or understand what exactly a translator is doing. It is not *translatio*—a workmanlike communication of language-independent content—except in the case of businesslike, technical translation or interpretation, and even there, a case like literal spoken medical or legal interpreting (e.g., accompanying a Spanish or Arabic speaker into a French- or English-language courtroom or doctor's office) is

17. Or at least their translated status seems less important from the perspective of English speakers, even as translation into English, and only into English, becomes ever more crucial to writers in other languages. In 2021, an international group of translators from German, including me, was told by more than one publisher in Berlin that translation into English is now overwhelmingly the gatekeeper for foreign translations in general. A book's foreign rights might sell to five or six languages not including English but would never sell to twenty or twenty-five languages except on the back of the English. I heard stories of sending a book to a foreign publisher, being told that they're reading and strongly

understood as conveying a person's experience, their person-hood, not just informational content. It is hard to accept the soaring claims for German Romantic *traductio*—the impossi-ble re-creation of form in entirely different words, indeed the mystical transfer of an original author's quasi-biological rela-tionship to their "mother tongue," "fatherland," and "national spirit"—but at the same time our descriptions of translation rely on that framework: describing "domesticating" transla-tion as "ethnocentric" presupposes a primal bond between language and ethnicity. And although translation is said to be impossible, it also seems when reading Venuti and others that the translator is weirdly omnipotent: with a wave of her wand she can assimilate the source text to dominant cultural values! As if it's easy! The original, meanwhile, is powerless to resist the crushing ethnocentric reduction of the all-powerful domesticating translator.

All the while, the first of Berman's three terms, *traditio*, continues to operate as well. Modern *translatio* and its inter-changeability of content worked to destroy traditionality and traditions, but *traductio*-translation restores many of the

---

considering it, then six or twelve months go by, and when the book gets a strong review in the *Guardian* or the *New Yorker* that same publisher emails the Ger-man foreign-rights office and says they're interested, can they have a look? This was much, much more the case in 2021 than it had been even a few years before. Aside from giving British and American editors outsize influence, this preference means that a book better suited to and potentially more successful in a market besides English might never get published there. And in the long run, everyone around the world will start writing and publishing with an eye to British and American tastes.

quasi-biological dynamics of tradition: as the re-creating of a form, it always posits an authoritative original work that "engenders" later versions which ensure that work's "survival." More fundamentally, the model of *traditio* highlights that debates about translation are really debates, or genuine struggles, about authority, as I will discuss in more detail in chapter 7.

No one, as far as I know, advocates a return to "pure" *translatio* or *traductio*, as if we were in the fourteenth or sixteenth century, nor a complete acceptance or rejection of German Romantic ideas about language, self, race, and nation, much less a return to Roman imperial ideas of authority. This palimpsestic history of "translation" sheds light on where some of the contradictions in our thinking come from but doesn't especially help us resolve them.

2

REALIGNMENT AND STRANGENESS

To move past the framework of sources and targets, whether what we ferry from one to the other is thought to be authority, content, form, or national greatness, we can begin by pointing out that Schleiermacher was primarily considering a specific kind of translation: from a classical dead language into a modern European one. Here the author and the reader really are "separated persons": no one grows up bilingual or bicultural in modern German and ancient Greek—they're thousands of years apart. That is indeed a gap. This is the context for Schleiermacher's defining the two methods of translation, which then get generalized to translation as such.

For a very different case, consider the Septuagint: the translation of the Jewish scriptures into Greek in the second and third centuries BCE and "easily the most significant translation in human history," as Denis Feeney writes in *Before Greek*, because "Christianity could never have developed outside

Palestine" without this earlier translation of the Hebrew Bible and prophecies "into the *lingua franca* of Greek."[1] Both ancient and modern scholars have tended to describe this event as if some Greek king commissioned a translation into Greek so he could have access to this important piece of world literature, but that's not actually what happened: the translation was done by Greek-speaking Jews in Alexandria "whose ability to read their Hebrew or Aramaic texts was becoming less and less secure." They were *pushing* their own texts into Greek, you might say, not pulling or bringing something into Greek from elsewhere.

So is this "domesticating" or "foreignizing"? It's neither. There aren't two separate source and target contexts in the first place. In Feeney's words: "The translation was not so much a transference from one culture into another as an internal realignment within an already multilingual and heterogeneous religious community."

We can think of this diverse community as replacing both the idea of a monolithic source culture and the idea of a monolithic target culture. The question of whether to domesticate or foreignize exotic kinds of food, for example, rests on the assumption that the target audience is all "monolingual English" with no special cultural expertise. (The assumption that readers don't already know what eba is.) That is a falsely flat and homogenous picture. An English translation of, say,

1. Denis Feeney, *Beyond Greek: The Beginnings of Latin Literature* (Harvard University Press, 2016), pp. 23–24.

a Cuban novel is likely to be read by lots of people who also know Spanish, who are maybe from Cuba, or are the children of Cuban immigrants, or at least know the basics of Cuban cooking. Junot Diaz's novel *The Brief Wondrous Life of Oscar Wao*, with all its Spanish and Spanglish, isn't "foreignizing," because bilingual Dominican Americans are no less "domestic" an audience than monolingual English speakers are.

If we generalize from this kind of case, we have the translator not as a lone mediator bringing two "completely separated persons" together, in Schleiermacher's words, but as someone writing within an already multilingual community.

Now, I'm not trying to bring my apples to put next to Schleiermacher's oranges and say, Let's talk about what I want to talk about, not what he wants to talk about. Even Schleiermacher's ideal case of drastically separated readers and writers involves a multilingual context. The choice facing a translator is not in fact between making the *Odyssey* or the *Symposium* sound like it was written in German or else giving the German reader the same feeling that the ancient Greeks got from the original, as it's sometimes mischaracterized: Schleiermacher says (emphasis added) that the good translator "seeks to impart to the reader the same image, the same impression, that *he himself* received thanks to knowing the original language." In other words, the choice isn't between modern German and ancient Greek—there's no time travel. It's between the monolingual German reader and the classically trained bilingual German gentleman, with all the gender and class relations implied by that term.

The good translator "gives the reader the same image and the same delight that reading the work in the original language would afford any man educated in such a way that we tend to call him, in the best sense of the word, an amateur and connoisseur, well acquainted with the foreign language while it nevertheless remains always foreign to him." That's Schleiermacher's model. And note all the language of privilege here: "educated," "connoisseur," "well acquainted," and for that matter "man."

Meanwhile, someone had to teach this gentleman-translator Greek in the first place; someone has to have published or collected editions of the Greek text that he would have access to; Greek had to be one of the languages taught and valued in German culture, and some of the people judging his translations will be readers and reviewers who can read the original, and there is also a preexisting tradition of translations from the Greek which the translator will be responding to in one way or another, and maybe the German language itself has been shaped by that tradition. *All* of this preexisting exposure is what a framework of separated source and target languages leaves out. And then, insofar as the translator and the reader share a language and culture—which they have to, otherwise the reader wouldn't be able to read the translation—the reader is going to be part of this complex community too. Schleiermacher's monolingual reader of German exists in a context saturated with these same exposures to Greek I've just listed.

Precisely here is the problem with reducing Schleiermacher's distinction to domestication/foreignization. He has a complex account of the relationship between an individual and his culture, while the domestic/foreign polarity assumes that anyone reading in English is part of a monolithic "domestic culture" while anything written in, say, Igbo is part of an equally monolithic "foreign culture." Recall the Venuti quote about translation as "an ethnocentric reduction of the foreign text to target-language cultural values": for this to even be possible, the original text must be intrinsically "foreign," not in a known tradition, not more or less familiar to anyone but the translator, not more or less cross cultural, while the translation, expressing solely "target-language cultural values," is "ethnocentric"—defined by ethnicity, not just culture. Likewise, the claim that all translation is a "forcible replacement of . . . linguistic and cultural differences" implies that a culture can exist in its respective language only. There is no room in this account for many of the actual facts of complex cultures: multiethnic populations or individuals, non-English texts written in a globalized literary marketplace with an English-language audience in mind, English speakers other than the translator having complex or hybrid relationships with the original's culture, or any other crosscurrents like the ones I've described. (Even though Venuti himself wants to recognize and champion precisely such suppressed or silenced strands within the dominant culture.) The problem, as always, is that once we posit a conceptual gap, we can no longer conceptually bridge it, however hard we try.

Even cases where the original source is far more historically "separate" from the language of translation than Greek is from German don't fit the domesticating/foreignizing paradigm. Susan Brind Morrow's recent visionary retranslations of the Pyramid Texts, the Egyptian hieroglyphics found carved inside the small pyramids at Saqqara, show how centuries of earlier translations were shaped, marred, by Orientalist assumptions. Two modern prejudices were constantly "being superimposed on the Egyptian original," Morrow writes: "The first is that the writing is primitive. The second is that it contains a myth." Translations made under these preconceptions cast Egyptian religious thought as "alien and incomprehensible, . . . ugly and stupid." The latest translation, fully accepted in mainstream Egyptology—from as recently as 2005!—featured language like "Pull back, Baboon's penis! Open, [sky's door! / You sealed door, open a path for Unis] on the blast of heat where the gods scoop water. / Horus's glide path—TWICE . . . Unis's anus on Unis's back and Unis's back-ridge on Unis's head." Morrow, reading and writing in a new context—she cites Pound, Eliot, Dickinson; she is herself a twenty-first-century poet—both humanizes the ancient Egyptian authors (as noninsane people who wouldn't produce something like this for such an obviously meaningful site) and reads what they wrote as "complex, interrelated poetic verses. . . . The astonishingly naturalistic hieroglyphs that comprise the Pyramid Texts belong to the realm of empirical observation that is the basis of both science and poetry."[2]

2. Susan Brind Morrow, *The Dawning Moon of the Mind* (Farrar, Straus and Giroux, 2015), pp. 10–13; James P. Allen, *The Ancient Egyptian Pyramid Texts*

My point here is that it makes no sense to shoehorn either the earlier versions or hers into being "domesticating" or "foreignizing": both are modern constructs in modern contexts, based on assumptions about what it means to be Egyptian, to be ancient, and to be a poet, and neither exists outside its present-day contexts as a simply better or worse transportation of unchanging original material.

Rather than beginning from an assumption of two separated contexts, we should view the translator as someone in a diverse community who reads a text in one language and produces a text in a different language. Following Feeney, I call this "realignment" within a single existing context. This model of translation without sources and targets encompasses more kinds of translation, like the Septuagint case; it describes translation in a way that better fits the practice of literary translators in the real world; and it welcomes sensitive attention to different registers in language without forcing them into a polarity of foreign = good, domestic = bad.

(Society of Biblical Literature Press, 2005), p. 60. Here is Morrow's astoundingly different translation of these same lines as actual religious poetry, describing a dawn in mid-July when Sirius rising signals the rising waters of the Nile (p. 97; see also p. 29):

> Say the words:
> The sword of Orion opens the doors of the sky.
> Before the doors close again the gate to the path
> over the fire, beneath the holy ones as they grow dark
> As a falcon flies as a falcon flies, may Unis rise into this fire
> Beneath the holy ones as they grow dark.

If translation is realignment, *what* specifically is getting realigned? Our perceptions, our literary categories, our languages? I would say it's the text's relationship to its audience—who is speaking, who is addressed, where the text is "pointing." *Any* text can, and any good text will, redirect our perceptions, redefine the genre it's working within, and change the resources or enlarge the scope of the language it's written in, but the particular "realignment" that takes place in translation refers to the vector pointing from author to reader.

One advantage of describing translation as realignment is that it makes it much easier to see the continuities between translation and monolingual relationships. Jonathan Franzen's novel *Freedom* was influenced by *War and Peace*, while *War and Peace*, translated by Constance Garnett or anyone else, is a novel very, very heavily influenced by the Russian novel *Voyna i mir*, by Lev Tolstoy. These two books in English, the one by Franzen and the one credited to Tolstoy, both influenced by Tolstoy's Russian book, are on the same spectrum of possible levels of influence and not even at the farthest ends of it. The full range runs from genre conventions—for instance, "the realist novel" (any realist novel in the twentieth or twenty-first century will bear some traces of Tolstoy's influence)—to influence in the usual sense, like Tolstoy's on Franzen, past adaptations like fan fiction and movie versions, to translations like Garnett's, and farther past that to even more heavily influenced texts, such as abridgments, or audiobook recordings in the original language.

Translation is unlike the other cases listed here because it involves a second language, but there are some kinds of analysis where this particular difference makes a difference and others where it doesn't. In a general discussion of giving an interpretation of or take on an original, the fact that the translation is in a different language is more of a technicality, and it makes sense to describe translation in a way that doesn't assign it to an entirely different realm of activity. Movie adaptations and audiobooks are unlike the other cases too, in that they involve, in different ways, a change of medium. Each type of influence has its own particularities.

If what the source text does is "influence" the translation, we would also ideally like an active verb for what the translator is doing: that translator is hardly a passive participant, so we wouldn't want to be stuck with them "being influenced by" the source text. I would say that the translator "takes up" the source text. If I were inventing from scratch my own word with a Latin etymology, I wouldn't call it *trans-latio*—I'd call it "accuperation," "taking up." But I'm not going to pretend that "accuperation" is a real word—I will stick to "translation," although sometimes refer to "taking up" as what the translator is doing.

There are many ways of taking up what someone else says: you can answer the question, continue the conversation, jot down notes on the information, react violently to the insult, grasp the argument, transcribe the testimony, flirt back, duck, and much more. There are different ways to take up what someone else has written: this is the complex set of activities known as *reading* (and responding). Reading can be defined as "taking up a written text." Translation is a kind of reading.

And an underappreciated aspect of the translator's experience is that, subjectively speaking, nothing we read is *foreign*. When I sit down on a park bench to read a book in German, as I have been known to do, it's not foreign to me—if it were, I couldn't read it! What I'm doing is essentially no different from reading a book in English, or rather it may be different, but it needn't be. The text I'm reading may be from an alien perspective, or with difficult vocabulary and syntax, or hard to understand for some other reason, it might challenge my assumptions and widen or narrow my horizons, but all these things might likewise be true if the text is in English. Reading encompasses many different practices—I can be reading for fun, as homework, to write a review, to change my life, to figure out how to connect a printer—and me reading in German covers the same range of possibilities as me reading in English. (I suppose it's not quite the same range: I might be reading something in German to practice or improve my German. Then again, I might be reading in English to accomplish the analogous goal of improving my English; there are some books I read in English and look up words from in the dictionary, others I don't.) In the experience of reading, a language isn't foreign.[3]

3. One place I've seen this point made, explicitly about the translator rather than the reader, is in an essay by Michael Emmerich: "When a translator sits down at her computer to translate, she is alone. There is no communication happening. Indeed, there is no transfer of a message *from* one language *into* another, because

* * *

The insight that reading takes place within a complex and diverse context and that translation realigns a text already in that context can actually be found in many writings about translation, even Schleiermacher's and Venuti's, with the help of one little retranslation. Schleiermacher's German word for "foreign" is *fremd*: a word that often poses a difficult translation problem. I personally have trouble with it whenever I run across it in a German text I'm translating. Like the English word "alien"—rarely an ideal word in a text that isn't science fiction—*fremd* means both "foreign" (from elsewhere, from another country) and "strange" (unusual, unexpected); its opposite is either local/native or familiar. The problem, of course, is that the objective reality of coming from elsewhere does not always coincide with a subjective feeling of apparent otherness. When someone or something is described as *fremd* in a German text, I often don't know whether to translate the word as *foreign, unusual,* or *disturbing,* or to give up and go with *alien.* For some people,

---

from the perspective of the translator at the precise moment she is translating, she is not between languages, and her languages are not separate. We might say, rather, that she is saturated with two languages—that she is a node for two languages" He calls the translator "not a bridge" but "something like a ghost." "Beyond, Between: Translation, Ghosts, Metaphors," in *In Translation: Translators on Their Work and What It Means,* ed. Esther Allen and Susan Bernofsky (Columbia, 2013), p. 50.

   The whole idea that reading in a "foreign language" is intrinsically and fundamentally different from reading in one's "mother tongue" is part of the ideology of "monolingualism," put in historical context and criticized in Yasemin Yildiz, *Beyond the Mother Tongue.*

what is *fremd* is not *fremd* (foreign things don't make them uncomfortable); for others, what is *fremd* is not *fremd* (feelings of alienation are not unfamiliar to them). Sometimes the nonforeign can be strangest of all: the call may be coming from inside the house. Emily Wilson wrote of her version of Homer's *Odyssey* that "I have tried to make my translation sound markedly poetic and sometimes linguistically distinctive, even odd. But I have also aimed for a fresh and contemporary register. The shock of encountering an ancient author speaking in largely recognizable language can make him seem more strange, and newly strange."[4]

In English, the two semantic realms of "foreign" and "unfamiliar" are distinct. They come closest to overlapping in the noun *stranger*, but even a stranger is not necessarily stranger than anyone else, just previously unknown. In French, meanwhile, the equivalent to *fremd* has close to the same double meaning as in German: *étrange*, cognate with "strange," means both the strangeness of the unfamiliar and the foreignness of the stranger. Camus's novel *The Stranger*, also translated as *The Outsider*, is *L'étranger*; both English translations of the title arguably overplay the main character's foreignness (he in fact belongs to the national community: a Frenchman in Algeria, which was then part of France) and understate his oddity, his indifference and lack of connection to other people. Camus's title could be translated equally literally as *Alienation* or *Detachment* (since *The Alienated Man* or *The Detached Person* don't work). In a point of slight deviation from German,

4. Homer, *The Odyssey*, tr. Emily Wilson (Norton, 2018), pp. 87–88.

one definition of *étranger* in the French-English dictionary is "unconnected (with)": something *étranger à la question* is "irrelevant to the question, beside the point." German, on the other hand, unlike French, seems to assume that what isn't yours must be attached to someone else—it can't be free floating. Things that are *fremd* in German include an assumed name, foreign aid, the others' hands into which your family's property falls, someone else's rights you infringe on or affairs you meddle in—not rightly or originally yours, but someone's.

So, are original texts and good translations foreign or strange, *fremd* or *fremd*, *étrange* or *étrange*? "Foreign" often seems like the right translation when talking about translation, but not always.[5] Berman's definitive history of German Romantic thought about translation, culminating in Schleiermacher, is a book called *L'épreuve de l'étranger*, titled in English by its translator S. Heyvaert *The Experience of the Foreign*. Lawrence Venuti translated an essay by Berman called "La traduction comme épreuve de l'étranger" and titled it "Translation and the Trials of the Foreign," emphasizing the "experience" (*épreuve*) as something we undergo, something trying.[6] Mean-

5. I would like to thank my translator colleague Chris Clarke for first suggesting to me that "foreign" in the sense of Venuti's "foreignizing" might be understood as, in essence, a version of *étrange*. He draws different conclusions from the double meaning of *étrange*, though, and doesn't discuss the similar double meaning of *fremd*, so he shouldn't be blamed for the rest of my argument.

6. Venuti, ed., *The Translation Studies Reader* (Routledge, 2000), pp. 284–297; original French in *Texte* 4 (1985): 67–81.

while, the phrase "*épreuve de l'étranger*," as Berman tells us in that essay's first paragraph, is "the expression that Heidegger uses to define one pole of poetic experience in Hölderlin (*Die Erfahrung des Fremden*)." The German Romantic poet Friedrich Hölderlin's translations of Sophocles are remarkable for the extent to which they aim to present the Greek *as Greek*, as alien and foreign. These translations read bizarrely, to the point where some of Hölderlin's readers considered his translations evidence of his insanity. The foreignness in the home language produces strangeness.

Neither of Berman's translators into English quite captures the sense of *l'épreuve de l'étranger / die Erfahrung des Fremden* as "undergoing a strange experience and taking it seriously," but that is certainly an aspect of Berman's meaning. He discusses how a work of art is in itself strange, and how translation helpfully emphasizes, adds to, that quality of the original: "The native strangeness of the work is joined by its strangeness (effectively increased) in the foreign language" (note that "native *foreignness*" increased in translation would make less sense). Here is a context where "accuperate" would work well: the translation "takes up" the native strangeness of the foreign work. At another point, Berman beautifully calls difficult words in a text "the skylines of the strangeness of the work" (not, I think, "the skylines of the foreignness of the work"). When Hölderlin writes in an 1801 letter that "what is familiar must be learned as well as what is *fremd*. . . . The *free* use of *what is one's own* is the most difficult," this very deep point will hit differently depending on whether you think of *fremd* as "strange" or "foreign."[7]

In any case, it certainly doesn't make sense to call Hölderlin's translations "domesticating" or "foreignizing." Berman calls them "Graecizing" and "nativizing" at once, in a "double movement"—there is not a dichotomy—because Hölderlin uses etymological archaic German to represent with shocking literalness the Greek connotations and meanings. Even the names of Gods, meaningless today except as proper names, are subject to this double movement: Hölderlin systematically calls Zeus the German for "Father of the Earth," calls Ares "the Spirit of War," and so on, thereby giving the Greek meanings back to the names precisely by giving us the names in German.[8]

It is an illuminating exercise while reading Schleiermacher, and Venuti, and many writers on translation, to as it were correct *fremd/étrange* in English, mentally replacing each occurrence of "foreign" with "strange" and turning every distinction between "domesticated" and "foreignized" into a distinction between "familiar" (clichéd, predictable)

---

7. Quoted in Berman, *Experience of the Foreign*, p. 161 (which mistakenly dates the letter to 1804), from Hölderlin's *Essays and Letters on Theory*, tr. Thomas Pfau (State University of New York Press, 1988), with the German word translated as "foreign"; the newer translation of Hölderlin's *Essays and Letters*, tr. Jeremy Adler and Charlie Louth (Penguin Books, 2009), also uses "foreign," while replacing "familiar" at the start of the passage with the same words used later: "what is one's own." The German reads *"das eigene muß so gut gelernt seyn, wie das Fremde."*

8. Antoine Berman, *The Age of Translation: A Commentary on Walter Benjamin's "The Task of the Translator,"* tr. Chantal Wright (Routledge, 2018), p. 104.

and "unfamiliar" (surprising, alien). Doing so makes many of their claims truer. Pound's versions of Anglo-Saxon or the better English retranslations of Freud, while not "foreignizing" in any normal sense of the word, really are defamiliarizing. It's hard to see how merely reading a domesticating translation can make it more "foreignizing," but any good analysis of a translation, even of an insensitive translation, will indeed defamiliarize its relationship to the original. Making this mental substitution also lets the same criterion apply to writing in general, not just translation: bad writing is predictable, good writing is defamiliarizing.

This last term is from Viktor Shklovsky, who says that any work of art, by *defamiliarizing* (sometimes translated "estranging" or even "enstranging") our dead, clichéd ways of seeing, brings the world back to vivid life, or not *back* but *to* a new kind of life we haven't experienced yet.[9] This is a very

9. The translations of the term I am calling "defamiliarization" have a long and fascinating history, involving Bertolt Brecht's *Verfremdungseffekt*, originally from a 1936 article on Chinese acting, later central to Brecht's practice, and prominently translated into English as "alienation effect," although scholars now prefer "estrangement effect" to better signal that Brecht was influenced by Shklovsky. The Shklovskyan term—or actually, terms—were influenced in turn by translations from German into Russian at various times, under various Soviet ideological mandates; the different translations into English had their own relationships to the German, Soviet, and American contexts of their eras. See Douglas Robinson, *Estrangement and the Somatics of Literature: Tolstoy, Shklovsky, Brecht* (Johns Hopkins University Press, 2008), pp. 173–175, for a full account. The more recent *Viktor Shklovsky: A Reader*, ed. and tr. Alexandra Berlina (Bloomsbury, 2016), pp. 56–61, argues, in my view unconvincingly, for a straight transliteration of the Russian noun *ostranenie* along with Benjamin Sher's 1990 coinage "enstranging" (with the extra *n*) for verbal forms.

important point about the foreign/domestic dichotomy, and about Schleiermacher's and Humboldt's dynamic of national appropriation as well: the domestic, the familiar, *isn't* in fact self-evident or natural; if something is too familiar we can't perceive it at all—we can perceive only what has been made strange to us. We no longer notice that stone we've seen a thousand times—it has become basically invisible—but art, in Shklovsky's great slogan, "makes the stone stony" so that we can perceive it again, engage with it, love or hate its stalwart stoniness. At almost the same historical moment as Shklovsky's line, Gertrude Stein wrote, "Rose is a rose is a rose is a rose," about which she later said, "Now you all have seen hundreds of poems about roses and you know in your bones that the rose is not there. . . . I think that in that line the rose is red for the first time in English poetry for a hundred years." She defamiliarized the rose, made the rose rosy. Half a century earlier, Thoreau wrote that a scientific description chiefly interests those who have not seen the thing in question—"men of science merely look at the object with sinister eye, to see if it corresponds with [its] passport"—while the descriptions we like best take what we already know well and make it new again; he praises the writer "who describes the most familiar object with a zest and vividness of imagery as if he saw it for the first time, the novelty consisting not in the strangeness of the object, but in the new and clearer perception of it." I think of Francis Ponge's whole book about soap—its volubility, its enthusiasm, soap—and I refresh Shklovsky's description of defamiliarization once more, translating it in my mind as "Art makes the soap soapy."[10]

Something too domesticated isn't actually more accessible or approachable, it evaporates altogether—we just take it for granted until art restores its visibility. And perhaps translation is an art especially well suited for this task: while a great work of literature accrues imitations and clichés and a body of scholarship and analysis and CliffsNotes that may well smother it, translations of that work free it from its stodgy fame and make the stone stony again, precisely by putting it in another language.[11] A bad text is one that, in Berman's terms, lacks "native strangeness"—and when you translate it, nothing happens. The translation of a true work of art is significant because it reinforces and augments qualities already inherent in it: "translation is not a makeshift, but the mode of existence by which a work reaches us as *étrange*" (translated by Heyvaert as "foreign," but I'm not sure about that). As Wilson put it, translation makes the work "seem more strange, and newly strange." Like Berman, Shklovsky insists that any good text is *étrange* whether read in the original language or in translation: "Aristotle says that poetic language should have the character

10. The Stein line first appeared in the poem "Sacred Emily" (1913; published 1922); her comment is quoted from *Four in America* (Yale University Press, 1947). Thoreau, *The Journal* (New York Review Books, 2009), pp. 637–638. Ponge, *Soap*, tr. Lane Dunlop (1967; Stanford University Press, 1998).

11. Berman, *Age of Translation*, p. 92, commenting on Walter Benjamin's "The Task of the Translator."

of the foreign. . . . Poetic language is therefore a laborious, belabored, impeded language"—made surprising, unnatural, and defamiliarized.[12]

From this perspective, a translation is not so much an interpretation of the original text as its own special kind of strangeness-reinforcing writing. And indeed, bringing in Shklovsky's notion of defamiliarization clarifies the issue of so-called foreignness in translation and lets us describe it in a way truer to actual experience. When I'm sitting on that park bench reading a great book, it strikes me as strange and new— it defamiliarizes what it's describing whether I'm reading it in German or English, and whether I'm reading it in the original or in translation from a language I know or in translation from a language I don't know. Maybe this tends to happen more often when I am reading a translated (or older) novel than when I am reading a contemporary American novel from a context close to my own. Either way, it doesn't feel like I'm reading an analysis or interpretation of something else. I am taking in the book's *étrangeté* in its own terms, taking it up. Strangeness doesn't have to be brought from a "source" somewhere else.

12. Robinson's translation from Shklovsky's famous 1917 essay "Art as Technique" or "Art as Device," quoted in *Estrangement*, p. 126.

3

PERCEPTION AND AFFORDANCE

The best and most thorough account I have seen of moving through the world and encountering stones made stony again is in the realm of the philosophy of perception. And shifting to the philosophy of perception here, in a book on translation, is less of a swerve than it may seem, because perception is relevant to translation in three ways.

First and most obviously, reading is literally a kind of perception: you're seeing and visually processing words on a page or a screen, or listening to an audiobook or a storyteller, if you want to count that as reading. I'm not going to discuss this topic, even though I ultimately think it's relevant—reading isn't medium neutral; reading on a page actually *is* a different kind of perception than reading onscreen or listening, and that difference has effects that carry forward into the thinking and translating and writing you do. But that's not my topic.

Perception is also relevant on the other end of the process, because art, whether literary or visual, or in a more physical way musical art, changes how we perceive—it renews our perception of the world, as Shklovsky describes. Reading not only *is* perception, it *changes* the nature of our perception going forward.

What I want to discuss here is a third way that perception is relevant: it is a kind of analogy for reading, especially for reading with intent to translate. "When I tell new friends that I translate Icelandic," Lytton Smith writes in his "Translator's Afterword" to Ófeigur Sigurðsson's *Öræfi—The Wasteland*, "they almost always ask, So you must speak it really well? What I should say in response is that I hope I see Iceland really well."

The analogy with perception is meant to break our sense of a subject/object dichotomy, which structures so many ideas we have about translation. Perception is our most fundamental model or image of the subject/object split: the idea that we're in here, in our selves or skulls, confronted with something out there in the world that we take in, and that this distinction between inside and outside is how life works—what it means to be a person. I want to talk about the philosophy of perception in a way that will break the hold of that assumption: we *don't* perceive a world that is "out there," separate from us; we perceive and live and move *within* that world, as *part* of it. So too, what we read isn't "out there" until it comes "in here," and a text that we translate isn't being "brought" somewhere, from French into English or whatever—there's a more dynamic interplay in translation between self and other, source and target, author and translator. If I can convince you that there's no subject/object divide even when it comes to things like seeing a chair, then maybe you'll believe that there's no such split in reading and translating something someone else wrote.

The philosopher of perception who I think gets it right is Maurice Merleau-Ponty, whose magnum opus is called *The Phenomenology of Perception*.[1]

Now, I know "phenomenology" is an awful word. It's easy to stumble over. When I type it or write it, all those *n*'s and *m*'s in those little syllables, especially in handwriting with all those arches, usually slow me down and often make me skip a couple of letters. The shifting stress in the different forms (phenómenon/phenomenólogy/phenomenológical) generates a kind of confusion and hesitation whenever I have to say it out loud. Your mouth lurches back and forth in a really unpleasant way between the *e* and *o* sounds, which nearly but don't quite alternate—pay attention to your jaw as you say the word out loud: *phenomenology*.

And what does it mean? Zoology is about animals, geology is about the earth, but what is phenomenology? The theory of things, the study of stuff? It is not a useful technical term like "epistemology," which is arcane but specifically refers to a specific arcane thing. The meaning of "phenomenology" shifts

1. Which in English should be read only in the excellent newer translation by Donald Landes (Routledge, 2013).

around, because it always exists in opposition to something else, and that something else is different in different contexts.

All of this is too bad, because what the word is meant to describe is the opposite of vague and baffling. When Hegel wrote *The Phenomenology of Spirit* in the early nineteenth century, the term had a different meaning. In English, Hegel's book is also called *The Phenomenology of Mind*, with the last word, *Geist* in German, being notoriously hard to translate: "spirit," "mind," "intelligence," even "ghost." The German word *Phänomenologie,* on the other hand, is really easy to translate—you just plug in the equally opaque word in English. What Hegel meant by his title was intentionally an apparent oxymoron: tracking the outward manifestations of inner reality. *The Phenomenology of Spirit* basically means "describing the visible, external phenomena that express the spirit or idea." That is not at all what later philosophers, from Edmund Husserl to Maurice Merleau-Ponty to today, are trying to get at. They (we) don't mean external phenomena but the event of experiencing: phenomenology means staying grounded in real, lived experience and paying attention to what it feels like to actually be doing or living whatever it is we're talking about. You might say that what I gave two paragraphs ago was a phenomenological description of the word *phenomenology*: what it's concretely like in your mouth and under your hand, what using it feels like. It's a very vivid, down-to-earth approach, and I wish there were a more natural word for it.

It's no coincidence that there isn't, though, because "staying grounded in real experience" looks different depending on what that "real experience" is defined in opposition to. You can't call something "real" out of context, only in opposition to something else: if you say something's a "real duck," what you mean is different depending on whether you're saying it's not a decoy duck, or not a toy duck, or not a cormorant, or not tofu, or not like the scraggly pathetic specimen of duckhood on that other guy's farm—my ducks are *real* ducks. The meaning of "real" depends on the opposition it's in. Phenomenology is in the same way a rejection of other theories, so it looks different in different contexts.

In fact, perhaps the only difference between a "phenomenological description of something" and a just plain "description of something" is this stance of opposition toward an existing theory. Kurt Koffka, the gestalt psychologist, said: "For us phenomenology means as naïve and full a description of direct experience as possible"[2]—and "naïve" here precisely implies "bracketing or excluding some specific existing theory." Phenomenology is oppositional, like the "real" duck. The reason you do phenomenology is to come back and refute or correct the other theory, otherwise there's no reason to give a phenomenological description in the first place; if you're not in the grip of that bad other theory, the whole thing's irrelevant. So my description of the mouthfeel of *phenomenology* isn't ultimately a phenomenological account unless it's in a context where someone is saying, for instance, that the sound and spelling of a word don't matter. If my description lets me

2. Kurt Koffka, *Principles of Gestalt Psychology* (Harcourt, Brace, 1935), p. 73.

come back and argue that the lived experience of the word is relevant, then I'm doing phenomenology.

Merleau-Ponty's phenomenology of perception, then, isn't a theory or a set of scientific claims about perception—it's a collection of *reminders* that we're meant to buy into, because the examples are so good, and as a result we're meant to realize that the other theory we're in the grip of *can't* be true. Merleau-Ponty is mostly arguing against two specific theories: a Cartesian one, where "I think, therefore I am," mental states are primary and I build outward to construct reality, and a naïve-scientific one, where the Newtonian physical world out there is real and our inner life registers and responds to it. You could call these theories Intellectualism and Empiricism. They turn out to be basically the same theory from different directions, with the same problem: once you posit a gap, you can't bridge it.

For example, take the idea that when we see a chair, what's happening is that "stimulus" "comes in" through our eyes and we "process" it. There's light bouncing around in the world, and the light that hits your retina gets converted to information and sent to your brain, which then makes a mental picture of what you're seeing. This is the naïve-scientific or Empiricist framework. It seems self-evident, but Merleau-Ponty says: It doesn't explain anything, because how does your brain "see" a mental picture? Is there a little man in there with his own little retinas? You've just displaced the problem of how we link up with the world to inside our heads, where you can pretend it doesn't exist.

He gives several other refutations too, in different registers, you might say, depending on what he's arguing against
in any given part of his book. There are scientific refutations: Merleau-Ponty was much better informed about real
science and more receptive toward using it than most other
philosophers of his time. Experiments prove that we analyze
more slowly when we're tired, but we don't quote-unquote
"analyze" this kind of visual information more slowly when
we're tired—we still know right away that that chair is a chair.
Parts of the brain responsible for analyzing information aren't
activated when we see a chair: that's science from after his
time, but he anticipated the findings. He talked about how
people with damage to parts of their brain that do analysis can still recognize chairs, whereas other brain-damaged
people can still analyze information but can't recognize
things in the world.

Along with the logical argument about a little homun-
culus in our brain, and scientific arguments, Merleau-Ponty
also gives the argument from lived experience: when I see this
chair over here I'm not being confronted with "sense data,"
as philosophers like to say, which my supercomputer brain
then processes. (These splotches of color: Are they a table?
a sunset? my mother? Nope, it's a chair!) That's simply not
what happens. And the counterargument which claims that
"it happens automatically" or "unconsciously" is just a dodge,
which lets the scientist or philosopher *say* that it's happening
when it's not. What is actually happening is that I'm *seeing a*

chair—not photons, not sense data, but a place to sit. That is what seeing a chair *is*.[3]

Nor am I seeing a surface—"the front of the chair"—and then I have to logically deduce that it's a three-dimensional object. A chair, like everything else in the world, is something we see from one perspective and not all perspectives at once, because it exists in space, and we have a body that exists in space too. Seeing only one side of the chair isn't "partial" or "limited," because there is simply no better, God's-eye view that would let us "see every side of the chair at once": seeing *means* locating a thing in the world, in the same world as mine, thus necessarily in a position that isn't mine, at a certain distance, with a front and a back relative to me. The fact that this chair is in the world means that it'll block our view of some things (like a wall) and might be behind other things that block our view of it; it has a front and a back, and we can see that back by turning the chair around or walking behind it. If it's a different kind of thing in the world we can see its different

---

3. For an analytic discussion in an academic philosophy-of-language context of the status of these claims about what we "necessarily" do ("I see it as a chair, not sense data"; "that's what seeing a chair *is*"), see the title essay in Stanley Cavell, *Must We Mean What We Say?* (Cambridge University Press, 1969). For example, he discusses how we are to understand rules or facts such as the rule in chess that you must move the queen in a straight line, a.k.a. the fact that queens move in straight lines: "You CAN *push the little object called the Queen* in many ways, as you can *lift* it or *throw* it across the room; not all of these will be *moving the Queen*" (p. 28). This isn't just a guideline or principle of good chess playing, a strategy you can choose to pursue or reject (like "control the center"); it is a rule of playing chess, a fact about what chess moves are. There are likewise facts about what seeing a chair means, or is.

parts in other ways, for example by going inside it. When we walk down a street, we don't see the fronts of buildings, we *see buildings*—that is what it means to see a building, and if we want to see more of it we walk through the door.

Well then, the highly trained philosophy major might say, what about a Potemkin village or a movie set, where they're not actually buildings? This is where Merleau-Ponty makes a move that is intellectually very satisfying—he says that the illusion relies on the usual case. We wouldn't and couldn't call something an optical illusion except against the baseline of normal experience. Sometimes an apple is in a bowl and sometimes an apple is sitting on the table, and neither one is a problem—we don't say an apple in a bowl is a trick—but we say a Potemkin village is a trick because we normally see buildings, not fake façades of buildings. That's what the trick *is*. The case of the façade doesn't prove we see only surfaces; instead, our ordinary life is what makes the façade an exception.

This is so satisfying because lots of philosophers and scientists use some bizarre specific optical illusion or experiment to then say, "What you've thought was true your whole life isn't true at all." Even if we're convinced by what they're saying, it's unsettling and frustrating. Merleau-Ponty comes along and says, Nope, you were right all along, you really do see buildings.

Incidentally, we can make this same move with translation: The annoying claim that translation is impossible actually rests on the obvious fact that translation is possible and happens all the time. If there were no such thing as successful translation, mistranslation couldn't exist, because there'd be nothing we could say it's failing to do. When my cat meows, it's not a mistranslation of whatever I've just said, it's unrelated noise, and everything would be like that if translation really were impossible. Therefore, the existence of mistranslation proves the prior existence of translation proper.

I don't want to try to summarize all of Merleau-Ponty's insights and what he draws out of them—there are semester-long graduate courses on *The Phenomenology of Perception*. The main point I want to make here is that perception involves a kind of intentionality. In phenomenology-speak, "intentionality" doesn't mean doing something on purpose, it means that perception embodies implicit or explicit intentions—when I see something, my body is directed in a certain way, my actual or potential actions are pointing toward something. Seeing a chair doesn't mean: a physical object exists in Newtonian space and I, a disembodied gaze or some kind of analytical robot, receive information about it. Seeing a chair means: "Aha, there's somewhere I could sit." That is the basic level perception operates on. The fact that I can sit in it is what makes it a chair; I can't see a chair without being aware of potentially sitting in it; I recognize it as a chair because I've gone over and sat in such things before, that's how I learned as a child what chairs are, a.k.a. what the word *chair* means. I also know how to go about looking at the back of the chair or the bottom of the chair if that's what I feel like doing for some reason.

In other words, the intentionality isn't a feeling or a reaction that comes later. Just as I don't run through a mental list of all the things those splotches of color might be, I also don't calcu-

late what I might do with the chair *after* the stage where I perceive it. (So, this chair: should I throw it? eat it? walk through
it? Nope, but I guess I could sit in it!) Seeing a chair is seeing
something you sit in, and what I see over there is a chair.

This doesn't mean the chair is exerting mind control and
forcing me to sit down; there are all sorts of reasons why I
might choose not to sit there. Maybe there's a "Reserved" sign
on it, or I'm giving a lecture at a podium at the moment, or
I'm stretching my legs, or I'm paralyzed, or it's behind a rope
in a museum in the Bauhaus exhibit. Still, the chair in a way
"suggests" or "proposes" that we might sit there; it is the kind
of thing one might sit in, otherwise what we're seeing in the
Bauhaus exhibit would be a sculpture, not a chair. There is a
two-way interaction between my body and the chair—it, as it
were, calls to me, and I know precognitively, without thinking
about it, what bodily action I would have to take to accept the
invitation. The relation between my body and the chair is not
a mathematical one between purely physical objects in space
but, as Merleau-Ponty calls it, "a living bond."

The French language expresses this dynamic in a lovely way
with the word *sens*, cognate with the English word "sense."
There are four meanings of *sens*. First, one of the five senses
(touch, smell, etc.). Second, it means judgment or intelligence,
as in the English "common sense" or being "sensible." Third,
it means meaning, like the meaning of a word. We don't usually say "the sense of a word," we say "the meaning of a word,"
but we do talk about "the sense of a passage," or about a word
"in the literal sense" or "the figurative sense" (i.e., in its literal
or figurative meaning). Fourth, *sens* means something that

"sense" in English doesn't mean: direction or way. East or west, going the right way or the wrong way, turning a knob clockwise or counterclockwise, a one-way street, a sweater put on back to front: all these phrases in French use the word *sens*.

The word's multivalence is perfect for Merleau-Ponty. Perception with your five *senses* is an active act of the *intelligence* (not just passively receptive of information); it intrinsically involves recognizing the *meaning* of the thing (a chair is to sit in); and it is a kind of existential moving in the thing's *direction* (knowing it's a chair depends on a familiarity with such things, on the ability in principle to go over there and sit down). I know what to do with it. It's part of the world I live in. There are all four kinds of *sens* in my relation to it.

Another word that captures this complex relationship isn't French and isn't Merleau-Ponty's but was coined by an American named James J. Gibson. One of the bizarre facts of twentieth-century intellectual history is that an American scientist, a psychiatrist studying how pilots perceive planes taking off and landing—he worked for the US Army during World War II and helped develop visual aptitude tests for trainee pilots—ended up with the exact same model of perception as a French philosopher reading Heidegger and Husserl, even though they didn't know each other's work at all. If Merleau-Ponty leaves you thinking, "That all sounds good, but how is it scientifically possible?" then Gibson's your guy.

His major books, *The Senses Considered as Perceptual Systems* (1966) and *The Ecological Approach to Visual Perception*

(1979), are as fascinating and eye opening as Merleau-Ponty's. The "ecological approach" of the latter title is Gibson's terminology for how we share a world, where the seer and the thing seen aren't separated as subject and object but move within a system of "living bonds." Without summarizing Gibson's incredible work, I want to use a term he coined and just pretend it's Merleau-Ponty's: *affordance*.

"The *affordances* of the environment," Gibson writes, "are what it *offers* the animal, what it *provides* or *furnishes*, either for good or ill." (Gibson talks about "animals" to emphasize the ecological aspect—there are all sorts of creatures with different life-worlds in the same space.) "The verb *to afford* is found in the dictionary, but the noun *affordance* is not. I have made it up. I mean by it something that refers to both the environment and the animal in a way that no existing term does. It implies the complementarity of the animal and the environment." To perceive things in the environment "is to perceive what they afford. This is a radical hypothesis, for it implies that the 'values' and 'meanings' of things in the environment can be directly perceived" and also that they are "external to the perceiver."[4]

In Gibson's terms, a chair affords us the possibility of sitting in it, and that affordance is *fundamental* and *primary*. A chair is *not* first and foremost an object with a position in space that includes a surface more or less parallel to the

4. James J. Gibson, *The Ecological Approach to Visual Perception* (1979; Lawrence Erlbaum Associates, 1986), chapter 8, "The Theory of Affordances," pp. 127–143, quotations on p. 127.

ground: no, what it really is is a place to sit. That's the level on which perception takes place.[5] The ground or a floor is what we vertical flightless bipeds stand on—it affords us support. A mug is an affordance to pick it up and drink my morning coffee out of it, and if that's what I decide to do, I don't have to calculate the proper position of all my arm and hand muscles and the position of everything in Newtonian space: I automatically adopt the posture of picking it up; what I simply do is pick it up. (This is why I can grab a cup of coffee anywhere in arm's reach more easily and accurately than I can touch my fingertips to each other by holding my arms outstretched to either side and then bending my elbows—because that's what we naturally do with mugs and it's not what we naturally do with fingers.) A cliff affords us the negative possibility of falling off it. A friend is an affordance to say hello, among many other things. The world is not full of objects: it is an ecosystem of real and potential actions and interactions. To identify something, Gibson writes, "is to perceive what can be done with it, what it is good for, its utility."

5. Among the many precursors to Gibson's (and Merleau-Ponty's) account of visual perception as bodily, not just visual, there is William James: "Common-sense says, we lose our fortune, are sorry and weep; we meet a bear, are frightened and run; we are insulted by a rival, are angry and strike," but James argues "that this order of sequence is incorrect. . . . Without the bodily states following on the perception, the latter would be purely cognitive in form, pale, colorless, destitute of emotional warmth. We might then see the bear, and judge it best to run, receive the insult and deem it right to strike, but we should not actually *feel* afraid or angry." A person's actual perception, as opposed to a pale, colorless abstraction of perception, requires "sensate seeing" (*Principles of Psychology* [1890], vol. 2, pp. 449–450, quoted in Robinson, *Estrangement*, p. 124). The pioneering Swiss psychologist Eugen Bleuler developed the same ideas, known in his context as "associationist psychology," and passed them along to his student Hermann

So this gets beyond the subject/object split. The animal and its world are complementary—each beckoning to the other, intending something from the other. Gibson also points out that tools disprove the subject/object split because they show that the "self" or the "body" can attach to and detach from various "objects": there's no hard-and-fast border to what's "me." When we're holding scissors we've changed our hand's abilities, so now we're in a different dyad with the affordances of our environment; there are different actions we can now perform with sheets of paper, plastic packets, people we want to stab, and other things in the world. A guitar lets us make sounds in a different way, and then we can put the guitar back down again. While I'm holding the guitar, *it* isn't playing music—*I'm* playing music, but I'm a different "I" than I was without a guitar. My glasses don't see the chair, *I* see the chair, even if I couldn't see it without my glasses.[6]

To return to reading and translation, the account of perception at the center of Merleau-Ponty's philosophy, with its intentionality, describes reading as a translator: engaging

---

Rorschach, whose realization that our acts of perception involve the whole psychology and ultimately the whole self led him to invent the Rorschach test (as I discuss in my book *The Inkblots: Hermann Rorschach, His Iconic Test, and the Power of Seeing* [2017], esp. pp. 292–293).

6. As the examples of scissors, guitars, and eyeglasses indicate, tools are very different from one another. Wittgenstein in *Philosophical Investigations* is especially vivid and convincing about their diversity: "§11. Think of the tools in a tool-box: there is a hammer, pliers, a saw, a screw-driver, a ruler, a glue-pot, glue, nails and screw.—The functions of words are as diverse as the functions of these objects. (And in both cases there are similarities.) . . . §12. It is like looking into the cabin of a locomotive. We see handles all looking more or less alike. (Naturally, since they are all supposed to be handled.) But one is the handle of

with language as an ecology of Gibsonian "affordances" we move through and do things with.[7] Other theorists have also described the affordances of language: as speech genres, or language games, or rules of response, as I will describe next chapter. Just as there are relatively few things one does with a coffee mug, a question or statement or other use of language doesn't leave us free to pick from an infinite menu of possible responses; the "living bond" between a creature and the affordances of its environment is precisely analogous to that between the active listener and the utterance she will at some point respond to. There are lots of possibilities, but they aren't endless and they have a structure. One of the things we are invited to do with an utterance—one possibility an utterance affords us—is to translate it. And if we do, we are guided by the original, which proposes or affords us a large but far from infinite range of appropriate translations. To translate is to act on the kind of taking up the text affords.

---

a crank which can be moved continuously (it regulates the opening of a valve); another is the handle of a switch, which has only two effective positions, it is either off or on; a third is the handle of a brake-lever, the harder one pulls on it, the harder it brakes; a fourth, the handle of a pump: it has an effect only so long as it is moved to and fro."

7. Merleau-Ponty extends his theory of perception to language, both in *The Phenomenology of Perception* and elsewhere (especially in an essay called "Science and the Experience of Expression," in *The Prose of the World*), but while he doesn't use Gibson's term, his arguments basically treat language as a *tool* in Gibson's sense: an extension of the speaker's or writer's body, through which we have direct access to them and other people have direct access to us. What he has to say about language concerns the issue of access to other minds, not action. In this domain of his theory too, what's allegedly subjective or objective disappears into a lived interaction: in a conversation, he argues, we're not hearing words,

What do we gain by applying this language of "affordances" to translation? The point isn't to redescribe "knowing what words in another language mean" with a new philosophical term. The point is to get around the false dilemma of whether a translator (or translation) is or should be "free." We should stop thinking of translators as "free to choose" their translation: we are actually *guided by* the original in the same way that a chair "makes us" see it as a chair. Let me reiterate that not being free doesn't mean we're enslaved—in the end, we can translate however we want, much as we *can* use a chair as a table or a sculpture or a battering ram if we want, but we're prompted to see it as and use it as a chair, because after all it *is* a chair.

I intend this point about getting beyond the subject/object split as something personal and heartfelt, not as part of some arcane intellectual debate: when I'm translating I really do

we're hearing the other person; when we talk, we don't have thoughts in our head that we then find words to "express" out there in the world—having the thoughts and saying the words are coextensive. This account is firmly in a French tradition. Merleau-Ponty rarely mentions Proust, but Proust has a well worked-out theory along these lines about reading: he says that truth and real knowledge are unearthed in solitude, whereas socializing is a total waste of time and a terrible way to spend your life, but what's great about reading is that you get to experience other people's thoughts and ideas while still being alone. He calls it "this fruitful miracle of communication in the bosom of solitude." An essay by Georges Poulet written after Merleau-Ponty, called "Phenomenology of Reading," takes the same tack: the thoughts of a book "are the thoughts of another, and yet it is I who am their subject. . . . I am thinking the thoughts of another . . . as my very own" (*New Literary History* 1.1 [October 1969]: 55–56). I think these are good descriptions of reading and communicating in general—but reading like a translator is different, an act of taking up the language rather than communicating through it.

feel shepherded by the original, not as though I am forcing myself upon it more or less violently or arbitrarily. The question of how I "choose" which words to "use" in a translation feels to me a bit like asking what pictures I "choose" to see in my mind when I'm reading an Austen or Dickens novel. Or what I "choose" to see and hear in a given environment, when my eyes are pointed at a sunset or my ears are near a barking dog—this is the analogy with perception. I'm *not* choosing. The book itself, once I've decided to read it, is what makes me picture Mr. Darcy or Oliver Twist in a certain way, even if it makes other people picture these characters in different ways; I may notice different things than someone else about the same sunset or garbage dump we're both looking at, but I'm not *choosing* to see the sunset that's there, once I've gone outside and opened my eyes.

Am I saying the original text determines or quasi-determines the translation? Well, yes, that's what makes it a translation! How could something be a translation if the original *didn't* influence how it turns out? I can't spell out in detail *how* the original determines the translation, any more than Merleau-Ponty can lay out precisely the criteria that make a chair a chair—he can only remind us that we do, in fact, recognize chairs. I am reminding us that texts "ask to be translated" in a certain way, and when translators "respond to" a text, that is actually what we're doing. The text speaks first, making its own demands.

All the philosophical dilemmas about whether translation "reflects" or instead "transforms" what's in the original

need to be swept aside. This is exactly the dichotomy that
Merleau-Ponty's account of perception is trying to free us
from: are we "seeing" objects or "constituting" them? Empiricism or Intellectualism? Neither, because we perceive
things in a world we live in and have the power to transform:
a chair is something we can go sit in; a mug is something we
can pick up. One of Merleau-Ponty's many great metaphors
is that perception neither finds the world nor creates it: it
reveals it, which he expresses using the term *révélateur*,
the developing fluid for photographs in a darkroom.[8] The
act of seeing *develops* what's in the world, like developing
a photograph. Likewise, a translation "develops the photograph" of the original text. Translators don't simply "recognize" what's there, but nor are we "changing" it into anything
it isn't already, though we can be more or less aggressively
interventionist in our darkroom. As a translator I take up the
affordances of the original, moving through its world and
constantly invited to respond in certain ways.

In perception, we see what's really there in the world,
but *we* see it, and it's there in *our* world, the environment
of what we notice and care about, which is different from
the environment of any other person or animal in the same
physical space. Perceiving means activating (or not) the possibilities the environment affords us to move and act within
that environment; reading like a translator lets us take up (or

8. From a book left unfinished at his death: *The Visible and the Invisible*, tr.
Alphonso Lingis (1964; Northwestern University Press, 1968), p. 27.

not) the possibilities the language affords. Both processes are complex interplays of the self and the world, neither objective nor subjective. We read the book itself, but *we* read it, from a particular perspective, moving through it in a particular way. And a translation both is and isn't the same as the original—it's the translator's path through it.

4

BASELINE AND CONSTELLATION

The discussion of "strangeness" in chapter 2 can be recast, from a phenomenological perspective, in terms of deviation from a "baseline." The Potemkin village is a trick, the mistranslation fails to be a translation, only against the baseline of normal experience. But from a phenomenological perspective—and many scientific experiments have proved this as well—all perception is differential: we see and hear and feel not things in isolation but only what stands out from the rest of the environment.

As Gibson analyzes at great length in *The Ecological Approach to Visual Perception*, optical information is not what the world, as it were, "communicates" to us ("Why should the world speak to us?" he remarks). Visual stimulation is not a signal to be interpreted; perception is not a process of receiving information. Instead, perception involves what Gibson calls an "ambient optic array"—a baseline—and "a disturbance of its structure." Movements in the environment, and the movements of the perceiver (who is never static—there are constant eye movements, if nothing else), create the dynamic occlusions and revelations, shifts in perspective, and changes over time that let us perceive the world. More precisely, changes provide one kind of information about the environment and nonchanges provide another; variations reveal what doesn't vary, while invariants of structure exist only in relation to variants. This is why perception is an act not just of the eye but of the living body: "a process of *information pickup*" always "involves the exploratory activity of looking around, getting around, and looking at things" (note the similarity of Gibson's "pickup" with my "taking up"). We don't just aim our eyes and take a single snapshot of something once and for all—we engage with the world. This also means that the environment we see-at-the-moment is not the environment we see: seeing involves holding in mind various past and present states of the ambient array, so that changes over time can be processed. We don't just see what's in front of our eyes, we see its difference from other objects and perspectives; we don't see the front of a chair, we see a chair, and that means perceiving the potential or actual past and future experiences in which we turn it over or walk around it. As Gibson forcefully puts it: "What we perceive is the world," not "the optically uncovered surfaces of the world at this point of observation."

Likewise, what Shklovsky calls defamiliarization can take place only in contrast to what is familiar to a given reader at a given time: "a work of art is perceived against a background

of and by association with other works of art." Reading too is
an act of "differential experiencing," which Shklovsky understands very much in terms of the science of perception: he
calls true art, defamiliarizing art, "irritating," borrowing from
physiology the term for a stimulus or nerve excitation.[1]

Shklovsky argues that a nonnative speaker can never fully
understand a poem in another language because "the slight-
est aberrations from the norm in the choice of expressions, in
the combinations of words, in the subtle shifts of syntax—all
of this can be mastered only by someone who lives among the
natural elements of his language, by someone who, thanks to
his conscious awareness of the norm, is immediately struck,
or rather, irritated by any deviation from it." And "the domain
of the norm in a language extends far beyond this," to every
nuance of sound and imagery, expression and style. Leaving aside his assumption that nonnative speakers can never
attain this level of mastery, his point is that we don't simply
read what's there—we read against a baseline of the norms,

1. The term "differential experiencing" is from Broder Christiansen's German
book *The Philosophy of Art* (1909), translated into Russian by G. P. Fedotov in
1911 and thence deeply influential on the Russian formalists, including Shklovsky.
Christiansen for his part had certainly read William James and probably Eugen
Bleuler; see chapter 3, note 5. Douglas Robinson (*Estrangement*, pp. 122–126)
quotes Shklovsky's essays which cite Christiansen in Fedotov's translation, giving
Russian, German, and English versions of all the key terms—sometimes multiple
English versions: his own and Shklovsky's earlier translator's—and scrupulously
disentangling the various interpretations taking place at every step of the process.
I omit all these nuances here (the quotations in my next paragraph are actually
from Christiansen/Fedotov as quoted by Shklovsky), simply giving Shklovsky's
position (in Robinson's translations), which I take to be correct.

or "canon," of that language. And ultimately this is due to the science and psychology of perception, which lets us see only in contrasts. That is why what is familiar is dead: it has sunk back into the ambient baseline and is no longer perceived. It must be made stony again.

Reading with attention to the baseline of the language, as opposed to taking the language for granted, is reading like a translator. A text itself, even without being translated, takes up the assumptions inherent in its particular original language. How? How does the text push, or pull, against these baseline assumptions, and how does it *not* push or pull against them? Reading like a translator involves not only finding the original text's deviations, originalities, and treasures but also deciding what are standard aspects of the original language *not* specific to this given text, which therefore don't need to be expressed in a translation.

You don't have to be translating to read like a translator—a careful monolingual close reading can do this too. But unless you have another language to compare and contrast against, it's hard to get a sense of a language's built-in assumptions, they're so second nature. (Notice we're not saying anything about sources and targets here.) This is why translating—practice in reading like a translator—helps your monolingual writing: you will write with greater awareness of your own language and the conventions you're operating in. The only difference is that a translator has a sense of how an author is taking up *the author's* language, and then has to express that in *a different* language.

Let me give a concrete example here of reading and translating against the baseline. In German, it is much more common and normal to say "not this but that" than it is in English. In English, you'd say, "I want a cheeseburger, not a kale salad"; in German you'd say the equivalent of "I want not a kale salad but a cheeseburger," or "I want not a beer but a whiskey." You'd say, "The train leaves at not 6:00 but 5:30." In English this feels like a maddening little detour, but in German it feels like an earnest commitment to accuracy—you sort of slowly home in on the true situation because you care enough to keep pursuing it. In English we tend to just cut to the chase and say how things are, then give further details if necessary: "The train leaves at 5:30! Not 6:00, like you thought, so now we're running late."

My language here of not-quite-compulsion—"in German you *would say* this," "in English we *tend to say* that"—is the language of affordances. German and English afford different possibilities, offer different standard invitations to their respective speakers; an English speaker *can* take the maddening little detour, just like you *can* use a chair as a stepladder, but then that speaker is doing something noticeably atypical or, in more dramatic cases, bizarre. Reject the language's affordances too boldly and you might even be incomprehensible.

No one ever taught me this difference between the two languages, and in my years as a translator from German I'd never noticed it as such. A "not this but that" construction would come up in something I was translating, and in short

sentences I would just flip it around ("whiskey, not beer";
"5:30, not 6:00"); in longer sentences with more clauses,
the occasional use of "not this but rather that" in English is
fine, so it didn't stand out and I didn't notice it. Then I found
myself translating a novel called *Anniversaries* by Uwe Johnson, where the construction kept coming up so often that I
finally perceived it. Some sentences from my draft translation:

> Lisbeth was almost surprised that the New Star and Garter
> Hotel existed not only in the Grieben's travel guide but also on
> Richmond Hill itself.

> Francine came in with a gray bitter brew of tea that she'd
> bought not at the pharmacy but from an old man way up in
> North Harlem, a wizard with herbs.

> In the middle of the park is not only a stable for police horses
> but also a police shooting range.

None of these sentences is an especially hard translation
problem in its own right. You can flip the sentence around,
or expand out the syntax slightly, or downplay the contrast if
there isn't really a contrast. Respectively:

> Lisbeth was almost surprised that the New Star and Garter
> Hotel really existed on Richmond Hill, not just in the Grieben's
> guidebook.

Francine came in with a gray bitter brew of tea, and not from
the pharmacy—she'd bought it from an old man way up in
North Harlem, a wizard with herbs.

In the middle of the park there is a stable for police horses, a
shooting range for policemen.

But seeing so many of these examples pile up made me think
a little harder.

That's when I started to realize that this is part of the
general mind-set of the German language. The German for
"but rather" is *sondern*, related to a German transitive verb
meaning "to separate" (*sondern*), while the English "rather"
is from the comparative *hrather* of the Old English adjective
hrathe, with no other surviving cognates, which meant "faster,
more promptly"—as I said, English wants to cut to the chase.
German words like *doch*—roughly "yes, really!" over opposition, as well as a particle of insistence—reinforce what the
prevalence of *sondern* suggests: that the German language
embodies a whole different set of assumptions about conflict
and agreement, statement and admission, precision and effi-
ciency, dialogue and communication, than English does. We
don't have a word in English that functions quite like *doch*,
because English speakers don't interact with one another in
the same way that German speakers do.

At the same time, Johnson wasn't just using a German tic for
no reason—he was doing what any good writer does: pushing

the resources of his or her language to express a personal vision. There is no writer I know of with a more earnest commitment to slowly homing in on the truth than Uwe Johnson—that's *why* he uses this locution so often. He is scanning and piercing, digging and digging, looking and looking, with a kind of insistent, staggeringly articulate, sympathetic but corrosive attention. Saying "not 6:00 but 5:30" is truer to the way his particular mind and art work than saying "5:30, not, by the way, 6:00." So now we have a problem. We can't just blithely flip the clause around into standard English, because the construction is no longer just the German language—it's the author's voice, it's part of what we're trying to capture in translation.

The translator has to tease out what's an aspect of Johnson's particular writing from what's merely the default German baseline and then capture what Johnson is doing to and with the German language. A "not this but that" construction might be more natural or less natural in another language, meaning a writer in another language will sound different when choosing to use that construction or choosing not to: phrasing a sentence that way in English isn't the same thing as phrasing a sentence that way in German. Once we see how Johnson is taking up or refusing to take up the affordances of his language, we have to mimic that same performance with the different set of affordances that English offers us. We have to read like a translator, then reproduce what we find against a different baseline.

Another way to describe the "baseline" of a language—perhaps a more natural or literal description—is as the

"conventions" of the language: the kinds of things speakers of
that language naturally do and listeners or readers naturally
expect. These are what Shklovsky called the norms or canon
of literature, which we read against and which art defamiliarizes; in the case of language more generally, Mikhail Bakhtin
called them "speech genres": the "relatively stable" linguistic
forms, the types of things one can say in a given situation in
response to another utterance.[2]

Someone's utterance, while inviting us to respond, doesn't
leave us free to pick from an infinite menu of possible responses—it channels our appropriate responses, and our possible inappropriate responses too, into a relatively small subset
of all the words and gestures that exist in the world. We have
an extremely rich repertoire of speech genres at our disposal—
Bakhtin gives as examples "short rejoinders of daily dialogue
(and these are extremely varied depending on the subject
matter, situation, and participants), everyday narration, writing (in all its various forms), the brief standard military command, the elaborate and detailed order, the fairly variegated
repertoire of business documents (for the most part standard),
and the diverse world of commentary (in the broad sense
of the word: social, political)," as well as "the diverse forms of
scientific statements and all literary genres (from the proverb
to the multivolume novel)"—a repertoire so rich that we often
don't realize we are constrained at all. But there are limits, and

2. "The Problem of Speech Genres," in *Speech Genres and Other Late Essays*,
tr. Vern W. McGee (University of Texas Press, 1986), pp. 60–102.

learning a language does not mean learning grammar and vocabulary per se, it means learning the genres of what it is and
isn't natural to say and when and where and how.[3]

Others besides Bakhtin have used different terminology
to describe linguistic conventions. Ludwig Wittgenstein talks
about "language games," and in my view the rules of a Wittgensteinian language game are synonymous with the Bakhtinian speech genres of a given situation. The sociologist Erving
Goffman uses the term "rules of response," and as an especially witty and creative example in his book *Forms of Talk*,
he lays out a schema of fifteen categories and subcategories
of responding to the utterance "Do you have the time?" He
lists thirty types of response, including jokes; flirting; saying,
"Sorry, I don't speak English"; correcting an actor's line reading; being a smartass and saying "Yes!"; and actually replying
with what time it is.

Polly Barton's memoir *Fifty Sounds*, about learning the
Japanese language and concomitantly acquiring Japanese
"forms of life" (she deliberately uses the Wittgensteinian term),

3. He beautifully makes the point—extremely relevant for translation—that
anything we say, "with all its individuality and creativity, can in no way be regarded as a *completely free combination* of forms of language"; linguists claim we
have this freedom because they recognize only lexical and grammatical forms, not
other norms. As I argued in chapter 3, the analogy with perception understood
phenomenologically helps us get away from a vision of the translator's "freedom."
Bakhtin says that the more rules you know, the *more* free you are as a speaker:
"The better our command of genres, the more freely we employ them, the more
fully and clearly we reveal our own individuality in them (where this is possible
and necessary), the more flexibly and precisely we reflect the unrepeatable situation of communication."

is a beautiful account of how learning a language is far more than learning how to swap out words for crosslinguistic synonyms. Focusing on the "ability to spontaneously produce comprehensible sentences" (i.e., utterances that follow the rules, that conform to the speech genres, not just the grammatical requirements), her whole book is about how "the majority of this 'ability' relates to learning how to read conversational cues, to tuning into the rhythms of speech, to sensing and mimicking nonverbal behaviour, and to knowing when and when not to try to speak." Barton finds it "overwhelming" how physical, how bodily, she discovers the process of learning the vast nonverbal system of a new form of life to be: the linguistic aspect of language learning is only a small subset of "us[ing] every part of your body to read the cues of other bodies." Conversation is not, as we might imagine, "trading perfectly formed, pearl-like ideas between one mind and another," but because "the enmeshed relationship that exists between behavior and language is concealed from us," we wrongly view speech as "an impartial conveyor of meaning, standing discrete from . . . anything to do with real-life people."[4] Her account fits as perfectly

---

4. *Fifty Sounds* (Fitzcarraldo, 2021), pp. 86–88. Gibson's argument in *The Senses Considered as Perceptual Systems* is analogous in some ways: we don't see with just eyes, any more than we communicate with just words, but since our body's role in seeing (eye movements, proprioceptive factoring-out of the tilt in our head, moving around to gather visual information from different angles) is largely concealed, we take it for granted and thus misdescribe what we're doing. Merleau-Ponty too says that we misdescribe perception as "seeing and recognizing an object."

in Bakhtin's, Merleau-Ponty's, or Goffman's framework as it does in Wittgenstein's.[5]

Whatever label or metaphor we choose for this dynamic—canon and strangeness, ambient environment and differential stimulus, playing a language game by the rules, availing oneself of an acceptable speech genre, moving away from a baseline—it is the linchpin of my analogy between phenomenological perception and reading like a translator. A translation has to match this dynamic of the original text.

I have now described two different directionalities, or intentionalities, in a text. It is important to keep clear on the conceptual difference between the two, despite their overlapping in practice.

As I described in chapter 2, there is the act of communication from speaker or writer to listener or reader, or to an audience community in a broader sense (fellow Cuban American immigrants, Aramaic-speaking or Greek-speaking Christians, etc.). Translation is an act of "realignment," or repointing the arrow of communication toward a different audience; this image is meant to convey the directionality of any act of communication. The realignment of translation also doubles the

---

5. Bakhtin writes that the case of people "who have an excellent command of a language" but "often feel quite helpless in certain spheres of communication"—awkward in certain social contexts; unable to code-switch—is precisely that of someone with an "inability to command a repertoire of genres of social communication." They may know the language perfectly in a linguistic sense, but not in a practical, social sense. I believe Barton would say that they cannot be said to know the language at all if they do not know it in a practical, social sense.

arrow, adding another voice to it: the selfsame communication is now translator-to-reader as well as author-to-reader. Still, it is an act of communication.

As we have seen in chapters 3 and 4, there is also a kind of directionality inherent in the text itself, irrespective of its function as communication. A text has a *sens*, an intentionality, a way of moving through the world (moving in language, moving off from the baseline of the language) analogous to the way that we perceiving animals have our own ways of moving through the world (moving within the world that contains objects, other subjects, and ourselves).

To slightly reduce the number of arrows flying around my book, I want to call this second type of directionality by a different name: I will call it an *arc*. Picture a fountain: a jet of water shooting up from the ground, at a certain angle, to a certain height, scattering and dissolving to a certain extent into drops and spray. Unlike the arrow, which "points" at a reader or audience, this arc has no particular end point, target, or recipient; it is a trajectory, a way of moving off or up from ground level. The text as phenomenological trajectory is not first and foremost an act of communication trying to reach someone, but a use of language—English or Icelandic or German—which actualizes various potentials in that language. It is the text's (the author's) own way of taking up or refusing to take up the various affordances offered by the language, while the language is the baseline, the ground or launching pad for the text.

Translation, then, does two things and relates to language in two ways. It *redirects the arrow* that exists on a social, interpersonal plane, running from one person, duo, or community to another. The old audience is replaced with a new audience (speakers of another language). In this sense, the language of the translated text is different than the original language: for example, it is English instead of Russian. At the same time, translation *re-creates the arc*, fashioning a new text that incarnates "the same" movement, but starting off from the baseline of a different language. In this sense, the language of the translated text does the same thing—moves in the same *sens*—as the original text. This is how I would unpack the universally acknowledged truth that a translation has to be "the same as but different than" the original: different arrow, same arc.

Here is how Rainer Maria Rilke, in a 1922 letter, symbolizes this double nature of an artistic text. He first complains that writers shouldn't be expected—a common demand today as well—to go out and live exciting lives to gather material to write about:

> No one would think to elbow a carpenter, a cobbler, or a
> cooper away from his craft out "into the world" so that he
> might be a better carpenter, cobbler, or cooper; musicians,
> painters, and sculptors too are mostly left alone with their
> work. Only with someone whose work is writing does the craft,
> the manual labor, seem so negligible, so *mastered* in advance
> (everyone can write!), that people think he would immediately
> descend into empty game-playing if left too much alone with
> his occupation. But what a mistake! To be able to write is, God
> knows, no less "heavy labor," especially since the raw material

of the other arts comes already dissociated from daily use
while the poet's task includes a strange additional duty: that of
differentiating *his* word, fundamentally and essentially, from
the words of mere interaction and communication. *No* word
in a poem (and here I mean every last "and" and "the" too) is
the same as the identical-sounding word in conversation and
ordinary use. The word's purer accordance with the law, its
grand interrelations and proportion, the constellation that it
occupies in a line of poetry or piece of artistic prose changes it,
down to the core of its nature, and makes it useless, unusable
for mere interaction, untouchable and lasting.[6]

This is a beautiful description of the transcendent nature of
art. On the one hand, there is communication *through* or *in*
language, here dismissed as "mere interaction," and on the
other hand there is a constellation *of* language, poetic words

6. Letter to Countess Sizzo, March 17, 1922, in Rilke, *The Inner Sky: Poems,
Notes, Dreams*, selected and tr. Damion Searls (David R. Godine, 2010), p. 75.
The American poet and writing teacher Richard Hugo made the same point in
a more homespun register: "You hear me make extreme statements like 'don't
communicate' and 'there is no reader.' While these statements are meant as said,
I presume when I make them that you *can* communicate and can write clear
English sentences. I caution against communication because once language exists only to convey information, it is dying. . . . In [a] news article the relation
of the words to the subject . . . is a strong one. The relation of the words to the
writer is so weak that for our purposes it isn't worth consideration. . . . When
you write a poem these relations must reverse themselves. That is, the relation of
the words to the subject must weaken and the relation of the words to the writer
(you) must take on strength." He even ends this passage with the same reflection
as Rilke's on the poet's labor: "This is probably the hardest thing about writing
poems" (*The Triggering Town: Lectures and Essays on Poetry and Writing* [1979;
repr., Norton, 2010], p. 11).

sparkling in the sky. The task of creating a translation, like the task of creating any other piece of artistic writing (remember: writing as a translator is just writing), is to pull or shape the preexisting language from its baseline into such a harmonious system. What a translation has to match from the original is not the words—of course not, every word is going to be in a different language—but the interrelations and proportion, the constellation, or I would say: the arc.

At the same time, this passage helps us think more clearly about how the distinction isn't really true. After all, a poem *is* interaction and communication too, just a different kind of communication than ordinary conversation. Mere ordinary use does exist as a limit case: an utterance can be purely informational, and translation can apply to the arrow of communication alone—relaying the hotel checkout time in English from a Greek speaker at the reception desk to a non-Greek-speaking guest, for example. But the reverse is not true: there cannot be art without communication, arc without arrow. Ultimately, the poem isn't a constellation way up above the terra firma of the language—it is a linguistic object, which someone wrote (and published) and someone else reads. As they say about trees falling in the forest, if a poem rhymes in the starry sky and there's no one there to hear it, does it really make a sound? And the disanalogy with stars is that the laboring poet described by Rilke *put* those words in their glittering places.

Perhaps a better—at least a starrier—image for "arc" than a jet of water is a firework launched into the sky. Based on how the firework is constructed, what chemicals it is filled with, how it is packed, it will trace a certain arc and give off colors and sparks at certain stages of its trajectory, bursts that start and stop at predefined moments, visible in patterns—constellations—that were built into the object from the beginning. They might be useless, unusable for "mere interaction," but they are not timeless, unborn and undying, and they do not exist independent of people.

Given the history sketched out in chapter 1, we can see how firmly Rilke's soaring claims for art rest on the German Romantic fusion of language with the soul. His hymn to the poet's labor and the poem's constellation in the sky is practically an unintentional rewriting of Humboldt:

If you were to think the origin of a word in human terms
(which is plainly impossible, merely because the act of
pronouncing a word also presupposes the certainty of being
understood, and because language itself can only be thought
as a product of simultaneous interaction, in which one of the
terms is not able to help the other, but in which each must
carry out its own work and that of all the others), that origin
would be analogous to the origin of an ideal shape in the
fantasy of an artist. This, too, cannot be drawn from what is
real, it originates from a pure energy of the spirit and, in the
purest sense of the word, from nothing; from that moment on,
however, it enters life and is now real and lasting.[7]

7. Humboldt, "Introduction to *Agamemnon*," quoted in Berman, *Experience of the Foreign*, p. 152.

And it's not just about untouchable and lasting constellations in the sky—Rilke really means his personifications of language. In another letter, he writes:

> Poetry steps into language from within, from a side always turned away from us; it wonderfully fills language up, it rises to the brim—but then it never makes any further effort to reach us. Colors are slapped onto a painting but then they settle into it like rain into a landscape; the sculptor shows his stone only how it can most magnificently seal itself up.[8]

Here even more than in the starry sky letter, Rilke erases the concrete reality of human beings producing the language in question.

I go back and forth between two ways of thinking about all this. Sometimes I feel tempted to concede that any talk of "the language" and what it is or does is ultimately a mystification: all that exists are *users* of language. A language doesn't work in a certain way—speakers are pushed or invited to speak and write in a certain way. Conventions (rules, games, genres) exist only in the practice of actual people. You can't "change a language," because language isn't an object; you can only encourage, urge, or compel the speakers of that language to say certain things, and impose various consequences on them

---

8. Letter to Benvenuta (Magda von Hattingberg), February 13, 1914, quoted in Berman, *Age of Translation*, p. 58; the translation above is mine, from Rilke, *Briefwechsel mit Magda von Hattingberg: "Benvenuta"* (Insel, 2000), p. 83.

for saying other things—consequences such as being thought illiterate, vulgar, or inept, being genuinely incomprehensible, or literal physical punishment when we're dealing with censored topics or languages that are banned altogether. In my image of a text as an arc, the ground or baseline isn't really "the language" but the collection of expectations that readers have, the various habits and customs of speakers, which a writer can either go along with or surprisingly, confusingly, incomprehensibly go against. Similarly, no work of art "has" "a structure," pure and transcendent, existing up in the sky independent of how that work is seen or read or heard. Discussing an artwork's timeless structure is shorthand for describing the experience that an individual person has had or will have of it.

At other moments, I tell myself to have the courage of my phenomenological convictions! If a chair can invite us to sit down—if a chair is an active agent that affords us various possibilities—then so too can language afford various possibilities, inviting and expecting us to say certain things and not others. The chair is not just a dead thing, inherently meaningless until I project my uses and desires onto it. No, it exists in a living bond with us, and surely we can likewise say that language exists in a living bond with us, claiming its own rights, making its own demands. That is certainly how it feels, both to writers who experience a poem "coming to them" or a novel's character "telling them what he wants to do," and to speakers, who have the sense that one way of saying something (or for that matter, spelling something) is "allowed" and another way isn't, as well to readers encountering language in a new and surprising, glorious constellation.

In what follows, I will continue to quasi-personify or grant agency to languages: for example, "the German language" puts things this way, whereas "English wants to" put it that way, even though of course I know that that my sense of "English" is of my particular English, and different speakers and translators will feel that the language provides different affordances. I will describe translators in living bonds with languages they have loved and lost, or languages that oppress them, or languages they find inviting. And I will talk about the "arc" of a text—of the text in and of itself, abstracted away from its readers or listeners—even if, in literal truth, this arc is activated or perceived only by an actual person at the receiving end of the "arrow" of communication. I will leave it up to you, dear reader, how to take all of this: as shorthand, since ultimately I am describing how a text addresses its readers; as phenomenological reality; or in one way at some moments, in the other way at other moments. If I can have a wavering adherence to the German Romantic model, so can you.

Before turning to the second half of this book and its specific translation examples, there is one more point I want to make explicit: since using language means pulling against or arcing away from a baseline (or playing with conventions, following the rules of language games, and so on), single words are not the relevant unit of language. Rilke suggests this when he says that no word in a literary text is the same as the identical-sounding word in ordinary use; Polly Barton's whole book is about how language is made up of practices, not words. But the argument is most explicit in Bakhtin, whose essay "The Problem of Speech Genres" is largely about precisely the question of what the unit of language is. How, he asks, can it make sense to claim that all these so-called speech genres, from a drill sergeant's one-word "Halt!" to a triple-decker Victorian novel, are in the same category? Only by understanding them as examples of an *utterance*. That is why, in this chapter, I have kept saying things like "an utterance provokes a response," not that a word or sentence provokes a response.

A word is a unit of the lexicon, a dictionary entry; a sentence is a grammatical or syntactic unit, connected in various ways to other sentences the same person writes or says. Bakhtin dismisses these as cogent units of analysis, quickly rejecting as well various other syntactic or semantic attempts to define units of language (the "phrase," the "communication," the "speech flow," etc.). In reality, since language is always produced by concrete individuals in concrete situations, the one true boundary between units of language—not arbitrary, not an intellectual construct for the sake of linguistic analysis, but clear cut and real—is the shift from one speaking subject to another: the moment when one person stops talking and the next person starts. Bakhtin calls everything that happens between one such transition and the next an "utterance," whether it be a short comment or a large book.

And the important thing about an utterance is that it is always in response to something, and also prompts responses in turn. I would say: an utterance is always an affordance, always in a living bond with whoever will respond to it. And someone always will—even if the poem we read doesn't prompt an immediate verbal response, it enters our life and infiltrates our eventual interactions in some fashion. In Bakhtin's words: "Any understanding is imbued with response and necessarily elicits it in one form or another," even if delayed.

A single sentence or even a single word ("Stop!") can sometimes be a whole utterance, in which case it acquires the utterance's qualities of being communicative, responsive, and so on, and we might be misled into thinking that the sentence or word is what has these qualities. But Bakhtin insists that a sentence as a grammatical unit has no author, no speaker (even though an utterance that happens to be one sentence long does): "Like the word, it belongs to *nobody*, and only by functioning as a whole utterance does it become an expression of the position of someone speaking individually in a concrete situation of speech communication." Language by itself—the word or the sentence as a component of language—doesn't express anything or say anything; *we* say things with language.

In so doing, we act in the world, respond to others, prompt further responses, and join the social interactions of whatever sphere of human activity and everyday life we find ourselves in. We play the language game, participate in the ecology of affordances. Unlike words in dictionaries, unlike sentences as permitted grammatical constructs, utterances have what Bakhtin calls an "intonation": a *specific person* is using an utterance to respond and call forth responses *in a particular way*.

Words don't mean anything; people mean things with words. When someone says "Good morning," *good* doesn't always mean "good" (e.g., when this phrase is spoken with exhausted resignation the day after a disaster), and *morning* doesn't necessarily mean "morning" (when said with excessive brightness to a spouse who's slept in): meaning exists only in lived contexts, not in dictionaries. We are free to choose which speech genre we want to avail ourselves of in a given situation; we are also free to "inflect" that genre (sarcastically, enthusiastically, reluctantly, taking-it-surprisingly-seriously . . .). Some genres (flirting, novels) are more amenable to inflection than others (military commands, business letters), yet there is always a specific person availing themselves of that genre, with their own individuality: "there can be no such thing as an absolutely neutral utterance."

And if there is no neutral utterance, so too there is no nonneutral word or sentence: *every* word or sentence is neutral. It never speaks from any position, invites any response, or engages with reality at all—"language" does none of these things until someone uses it. Even when it seems that words themselves are expressive—with an "emotional tone," "stylistic aura," "coloring," etc. (the scare quotes are Bakhtin's)—in fact it is false to say that we choose our words depending on *their* tone; actually, *we* give them their tone, "invest" the word with what we are expressing, and choose it because "it can accommodate or not accommodate our expressive goals in combination with other words, that is, in combination with the whole of our utterance."

While an utterance has clear and concrete external boundaries (it is the change from one speaker to another), it has fluid and permeable internal boundaries: a complex or hybrid utterance will incorporate and inflect all sorts of simple, "primary" utterances. Lines of dialogue in a novel are the utterances of characters incorporated into the utterance of the novelist. An essay quotes or paraphrases others' arguments, supporting or denying or confirming or refuting them. As Bakhtin describes it, "The speaker's expression penetrates through these [internal] boundaries and spreads to the other [person]'s speech, which is transmitted in ironic, indignant, sympathetic, or reverential tones. . . . The other's speech thus has a dual expression: its own, that is, the [other person]'s, and the expression of the utterance that encloses the speech." This is most obviously true when someone else's speech is put in quotation marks, "but any utterance, when it is studied in greater depth under the concrete conditions of speech communication, reveals to us many half-concealed or completely concealed words of others with varying degrees of foreignness. . . . The utterance proves to be a very complex and multiplanar phenomenon if considered not in isolation and with respect to its author (the speaker) only, but as a link in the chain of speech communication and with respect to other, related utterances." If nothing else, any utterance uses words that have been used before, with collectively negotiated meanings—that's what the words of a language *are*. No speaker, Bakhtin reminds us, is "the biblical Adam, dealing only with virgin and still unnamed objects, giving them names for the first time," even if simplistic linguistic models of an active speaker and a passive listener might suggest so. Instead, language is "dialogical" and "heteroglossic"—spoken in someone's voice and always incorporating, responding to, invoking and evoking the "voices" of others within the very utterance.

Bakhtin is probably most well known in literary studies for arguing that fiction is inherently dialogical and that the novel is the form that best exemplifies this aspect of language in general.[9] Anything said in a novel is "double-voiced": all the language employed in a novel is simultaneously the character's or narrator's and also "accented" with the author's "tone" or "inflection." But translation is an even more literal example

9. See especially his book-length essay "Discourse in the Novel," in *The Dialogic Imagination: Four Essays,* ed. Michael Holquist, tr. Caryl Emerson and Michael Holquist (University of Texas Press, 1981), pp. 259–422.

Putting Bakhtin in the context of the history of translation I described in chapter 1 helps explain perhaps the most baffling part of his theory: his claim that while novels are multivoiced, poetry is inherently "monologic." How can he describe poetry that way? Poetry obviously incorporates, reinflects, and infuses a new subjectivity into prior uses of language; even in terms of the multiple characters of a novel, he has the example of one of the great novels in verse, *Eugene Onegin,* staring him right in the face.

I think the only possible explanation for Bakhtin's strange lapse in calling poetry "monologic" is a lingering German Romantic mysticism, like Humboldt's and Rilke's: the idea of poetic language as turning away from us, speaking only to itself. This Romantic idea of "a poem's monologic essence," of "the work as a self-referential, hermetic, monologic totality" (the quotes are from Berman, *Age of Translation,* pp. 58–59, in the context of Rilke and Walter Benjamin) must be why Bakhtin seems to forget that poetry works the same way as he rightly says all other language works. This is despite the fact that Bakhtin in "Speech Genres"

of double-voiced language: the translator's version of an author's text is very clearly a double utterance, spoken by both the translator and the author at once.

This is why I say that when we take up a text by writing a translation of it, something else happens to its "arrow" besides being realigned: it is doubled; the text now has two authors. When compared to the act of communication that was the original text, not only is a foreign-language writer now reaching new readers (their book pointed toward a new audience), but that book is *at the same time* a translator speaking to *her* readers, shaping her own brand, increasing her own profile, marketing the author in her (the translator's) own literary scene, expending her own social capital to get people to read

---

explicitly argues against a German Romantic view of language. He writes that privileging the word or grammatical sentence and neglecting the utterance downgrades actual responsive communication to a secondary function of language. The model of a "speaker" and a "listener" or "understander," which he traces back to Saussure, is misleading because the latter is assigned a purely passive role, while in fact "when the listener perceives and understands, he simultaneously takes an active, responsive attitude toward" what he perceives. (No one simply takes in language, any more than they take in the sense data of a chair—there is a living bond.) Ultimately, he derives the view of language as primarily the externalization and expression of someone's mind, "regarded from the speaker's standpoint as if there were only *one* speaker who does not have any *necessary* relation to *other* participants in speech communication," from German Romanticism: the same Wilhelm von Humboldt I discussed in chapter 1. And as we also saw in Rilke, emphasizing the fusion of language and a speaker's "being" makes it impossible to understand how that language is shared with others: taking as typical the case of a single, isolated person expressing an inner thought, not the case of ordinary communication with active others whose previous utterances and anticipated future responses are embedded in this one, places language up in the starry sky, out of touch with actual language use.

a writer they may never have heard of before, angling for her own prizes, and all the other interactions in the world that go with publishing a book. The translator's authorship does not erase or replace the original author's authorship, because language is always capable of carrying multiple voices in one and the same utterance. Voices are not mutually exclusive. (This isn't a hard argument to make: when it comes to movies, we are perfectly comfortable with accepting that the same scene or line speaks in multiple voices—the screenwriter's, the director's, the cinematographer's, the actor's.)

To think of what we translate as "utterances" sweeps away a huge amount of lexical analysis, because we don't translate words of a language, we translate uses of language. And yet, in talking about translations, it is almost impossible to avoid isolating a word or two and discussing how well or badly they were translated. I too will do so in the following chapters, even if, when discussing the translation of individual words, I constantly argue that we have to take the whole utterance (text) into account. Chapters 6 and 7 will then expand the scope, to what I think we actually do translate—the force of an utterance—and then to how we judge translations as a whole.

5

TRANSLATING WORDS

The translator's task is not to find the right word for a specific foreign word. English is a particularly rich source of examples that show this, because of its large and multilayered vocabulary—by some accounts, it has a much larger vocabulary than any other language, although it's not clear exactly how to measure that, or what counts as a word; maybe it just means the *Oxford English Dictionary* is really long. A waiter at a fancy French restaurant in New York may be supercilious, arrogant, haughty, snooty, or stuck-up, and no dictionary will tell you what's the right word to use in a translation because they all mean the same thing. Even the word in the original language, presumably one of a smaller range of synonyms, won't tell you the right word for the translation. Like proprioception—the bodily sense that tells us where our body is in space (whether we're sitting or standing, if we're balanced or about to fall over)—the translator's "ear" is used in making countless small adjustments; it's not a matter of conscious semantic decisions.

Along with vocabulary, grammatical forms can be more or less copious in different languages; I suspect that any language will be richer in grammatical nuance in certain areas and poorer in other areas. For example, there is one present tense in Norwegian and two in English: "I sit" and "I am sitting"—or, with a contraction, "I'm sitting." None of these three is a more or less accurate translation of "*eg sit.*" It as it were *looks as though* "I sit" is a closer or more literal translation of "*eg sit,*" but it isn't—each of the three English options is equally "close to" the original. When I translate Jon Fosse, who uses simple words repeated often, I have no choice but to make use of English's larger vocabulary and richer structure of tenses, so every time I translate "*eg sit,*" I have to make the decision that Edith Grossman reminded me to make: "I sit" or "I'm sitting"? The decision is based not on the words of the original but on the larger rhythm or music I am trying to convey or re-create.

Fosse writes long dreamlike scenes in which many events and time frames coexist in the present; he once told me about his *Aliss at the Fire* that he thinks "the structure of the book" is "clearer" in my translation than in the original, and I think this is because English, my English version of his book, uses the distinction between present and present continuous, unavailable to him, to navigate through these time frames. (Whether we want the translation to be clearer than the original is a

different question.) Here is a passage from near the start of
the book:

> ... the year is 2002 ... but then it comes back to her, how he
> disappeared, that Tuesday, in late November, in 1979, and all at
> once she is back in the emptiness, she thinks, and she looks at
> the hall door and then it opens and then she sees herself come
> in and shut the door behind her and then she sees herself walk
> into the room, stop and stand there and look at the window and
> then she sees herself see him standing in front of the window
> and she sees, standing there in the room, that he is standing and
> looking out into the darkness ...

The moments "sees herself come in" and "sees herself walk" (instead of "coming in" and "walking"), then "sees herself see him
standing" (instead of "seeing him standing" or "see him stand"),
then "sees ... that he is standing and looking" slide the reader
from a single perspective into a double and triple one.

Any word needs to be translated not as a word but as part
of a complex utterance. One example not from my own work
is Emily Wilson's decision how to translate *polytropos*, the adjective applied to Odysseus in line 1 of Homer's *Odyssey*: "Tell
me about a complicated man."[1] Is Odysseus here, introduced
as *polytropos*, "much turned" or "multiply turning," passively

---

1. She has discussed this many times in print and in lectures available online;
I quote from the profile of Wilson by Wyatt Mason, "The First Woman to Translate the 'Odyssey' into English," *New York Times Magazine*, November 2, 2017.

buffeted by fate or actively tricky and sneaky? Also, is he admirable or dubious? Is he prudent or adventurous, or just "a
straying husband"—another perfectly literal translation of
the Greek? All of the above, but then which do you want to
emphasize, and how strongly? The answer depends not only
on the meaning of the Greek, but equally importantly on
Odysseus's current reputation in the English-speaking world:
roughly that of a cartoonish superhero, with little regard to
the humanity and the challenges of the wife back home. You
then have to calibrate carefully how much bubble bursting the
readers with these preconceptions will tolerate without starting to see the translator as having an ax to grind—a translation
mustn't be too wrenching, and no one wants readers to shoot
the messenger or blame the realigner. Wilson herself calls the
straying-husband translation "radical," giving "an entirely different setup for the poem," and admits she didn't want to go
quite that far, but: "I wanted there to be a sense that maybe
there is something wrong with this guy . . . and that there are
going to be layers." Not to mention that she wanted to signal
to readers that they can relate to the character from a contemporary perspective, wanted the language to be modern
and colloquial, not stuffy and off-puttingly Poetic.[2] And also

2. As she writes in the introduction to her translation of the *Odyssey* (p. 83):
"In using language that is largely simple, my goal is not to make Homer sound
'primitive,' but to mark the fact that stylistic pomposity is entirely un-Homeric.
I also hope to invite readers to respond more actively with the text. Impressive
displays of rhetoric and linguistic force are a good way to seem important and
invite a particular kind of admiration, but they tend to silence dissent and discour-
age deeper modes of engagement."

it had to be in iambic pentameter. In the end—at least before she continued to revisit the decision after publication—she felt that "complicated" was the translation most "responsible about my relationship to the Greek text" and "the best I can get toward the truth." It makes no sense to think about her translation as true or not true to the word itself, to "*polytropos*" in isolation. It's complicated. As she wrote in 2019 in one of her many mini essays on Twitter about translation choices: "I often encounter the idea among non-translators that there are a (tiny) number of words that are hard to translate, and all the others are easy. That is not the case. We have to weigh every every trope, twist, turn and sound."

Reading, strangely, is no more a matter of individual words than translating is. My first published essay, from before I became a translator, was a personal anecdote about reading Willa Cather's magnificent novel *The Professor's House*, and how it took me the same amount of time to read the first forty or fifty pages as it did to read the rest. Why? There weren't harder words in the beginning, words that no longer slowed me down once I reached the middle and end—the English of the novel was not unfamiliar to me—and yet somehow, in a more abstract, holistic sense, I had to "learn the language" of the book, and after forty or fifty pages I had "learned" it. I had encountered this same phenomenon before, while literally learning German and attempting to read books in German; there too, though I looked up a lot of words in the early pages, I no longer needed to after forty or fifty pages. But Cather made me realize that this wasn't part of the process of mastering a foreign language. Since the author hadn't used up all of his or her vocabulary in the first forty or fifty pages, the initial slowness must not have been due to the words per se.

Nowadays, when I read a book in a language I know but don't know fluently, I can tell whether I like it even if I don't know precisely what it means: it doesn't matter whether I look up words or don't, I'm still reading the book. Strange, but true. This is a different experience than translating from such a language: when I translate Fosse from Norwegian, I am forced to proceed very slowly all the way through, looking everything up. The enforced slow reading is a different experience from just reading—one that luckily works well with Fosse's writing. I think that being forced to read him so slowly makes me read him better, more appropriately, something that isn't true for other writers.

But surely reading and translation must be built on—must rest on the foundation of—understanding the individual words? Not necessarily.

The oldest anthology of Chinese poetry—*The Book of Odes*, a.k.a. *Book of Songs, Classic of Poetry, Shijing*, from around the time of David's Psalms and Homer's epics—has been a mainstay of elite Chinese education for millennia, but the poems have required glosses and commentaries for some two thousand years. Classical Chinese lacks many grammatical markers (number, gender, person, tense) that help in understanding what's being talked about; to phrase it positively, not as a lack, what makes the language comprehensible is "the reader's perception of the context." The poem as a whole explains the words at least as much as the other way around:

> As [the early Confucian philosopher] Mencius (372–289 BC) said of understanding the Odes, already difficult in his own time, the reader "must not let the use of a word in it spoil his comprehension of a phrase, neither must he let the phrase spoil his comprehension of the intention; but he must let his thought go to meet the intention as he would a guest." In other words, he must start with some conception of the intention, confirming his hypothesis by all that is contained in the language used to express it, rather than by analysing the language first in order to discover the intention.[3]

We would like to think that understanding the words of a language is necessary and sufficient for understanding the

---

3. Arthur Cooper, "The Oldest Chinese Poetry," in *The Translator's Art: Essays in Honour of Betty Radice* (Penguin, 1987), p. 48. Another essay in the same collection—Wendy Doniger O'Flaherty's "On Translating Sanskrit Myths"— describes a late Rudyard Kipling short story that dramatizes the same point. In "Proofs of Holy Writ," William Shakespeare is hanging out drinking with Ben Jonson, the real-life contemporary who famously snarked that Shakespeare was poorly educated, with "small Latin and less Greek." A bundle of papers arrives by messenger, sent by the King James Bible committee, who, it turns out, have secretly commissioned Shakespeare to ghost-translate for them. Jonson reads the tipsy, brilliant Shakespeare all the earlier translations, and Shakespeare fashions one superlative verse after another, from them and his own intuitive imagination. He occasionally asks Jonson for the literal meaning of the Latin but then quickly interrupts Jonson's long-winded explanations and goes on to ignore Jonson's pedantic objections to his looser translations. The moral of the story, as drawn by Doniger O'Flaherty, is not that translators must be great poets—if so, "the Penguin Classics would be a slender set of volumes indeed"—but that the workhorse scholar, the Ben Jonson, "should give as free a rein as possible to the poet in him" (pp. 127–28).

meaning of an author—were that true, it would put human communication and interpersonal interactions on much more solid footing. In fact, these are two different processes. Polly Barton in Japan, mastering one of these domains, was far from mastering the other.

Perhaps it would sound less counterintuitive or appalling to put it like this: there are different ways to not know what a word means, and different actions you can take as a result. The philosopher Stanley Cavell gives an example: "Imagine that you are in your armchair reading a book of reminiscences and come across the word 'umiak.' You reach for your dictionary and look it up. Now what did you do? Find out what 'umiak' means, or find out what an umiak is?" It may seem strange that we can discover something about the world in a dictionary, he says, but perhaps this is because when we try to picture "finding out a fact about the world" we imagine a situation like asking someone's name and address, or looking inside a box. Or perhaps we imagine looking a word up in the dictionary as "the characteristic process of learning language," not of learning about the world. "But it is merely the end point in the process of learning the word. When we turned to the dictionary for 'umiak' we already knew everything about the word, as it were, but its combination: we knew what a noun is and how to name an object and how to look up a word and what boats are and what an [Inuit] is. We were all prepared for that umiak."[4] (Bakhtin would say: We know the speech genres of that book we were reading, and dictionary entries, and future

4. Cavell, *Must We Mean*, pp. 19–20.

sentences we will read or say about umiaks, and that is knowing a lot! Barton would say: We know the language.)[5] What the reader of a Confucian ode knows without knowing the meaning of a given word is very far from nothing; a translator's not knowing the meaning of a word he is translating is only one type of failure of knowledge, not the whole ball game.

My examples so far are of especially foreign bits of language—cryptic millennia-old Chinese poetry, Japanese to a young Englishwoman, umiaks to the bourgeois armchair reader—but what I'm describing is an aspect of reading, hence translating, in general. Marcel Proust, before *Remembrance of Things Past*, spent years immersing himself in the work of John Ruskin and eventually translated two of Ruskin's books into French. He was far from fluent in English—by some accounts practically unable to speak it, though he could read it—and he apparently overheard a nasty comment at his publisher's office about how bad his translation was no doubt going to be. Proust allegedly responded, "I don't claim to know English;

5. Cavell remarks that the task of properly "aligning language and the world" will look quite different "when (say) we run across a small boat in Alaska of a sort we have never seen and wonder—what? What it is, or what it is called?" This is precisely the translator's problem, even with objects we have seen and used but never named. I sometimes explain it to nontranslators this way: In an old-fashioned elevator, where there are the metal doors attached to the opening on each floor of the building and then the wooden slat door in the cabin that accordions into diamond shapes when the elevator operator slides it closed, what do you call that wooden slat door? I understand the German word that means this, but I can't find it in any German-English dictionaries. And how do I look it up in English, since I don't know what it's called?*

* It's a scissor gate.

I claim to know Ruskin," and in fact both French and English readers would later marvel at how well he captured Ruskin's meaning and style.[6] He collaborated with his mother and later an English friend, Marie Nordlinger, who provided Proust with first drafts in French which he reworked and reworked again, and there has always been skepticism about this process, or a sense that Proust was somehow cheating. But there is nothing outrageous or even atypical about what he did. Translators don't need to be bilingual dictionaries, they can use bilingual dictionaries. Fluency in speaking English is neither necessary nor sufficient for reading and translating Ruskin.

To descend for a moment from the sublime to the personal: Someone I know was once preparing to take her graduate-school language exam, in French. The test required you to translate a page or two by someone like Roland Barthes, using a dictionary; it was an intimidating hurdle in her department, generally felt to be very difficult, and if you failed three times you couldn't try again and you would be unable to get your degree. Several people taking the exam with her were on their third try. This particular person's French grammar and vocabulary were not great—she had lived for a time in France and could communicate in the language but had never made it past French 1—but she had heard me talk about translation and she wasn't worried. As her classmates anxiously looked up every word in the dictionary and wrestled with making

---

6. Jean-Yves Tadié, *Marcel Proust: A Life*, tr. Euan Cameron (Viking, 1999), p. 368; see also pp. 350, 400, 433.

the definitions fit together, she thought about what Barthes was actually saying, asked herself what he must mean, and wrote that down, not particularly worrying about the words. If the English is plausible, it's going to be a better translation of the French; perhaps, in this context, even a word translated wrong would come across to the graders as an interesting interpretation, not a mistake. I never saw the source text or translation, but I know she passed the exam.

Now, this point mustn't be taken to an extreme any more than its opposite. The eminent translator and writer on translation David Bellos gave a talk in 2020 where he addressed head-on what he called "the outrageous claim made by many otherwise quite sensible people that you don't need to know the source language particularly well in order to translate it. . . . *What are dictionaries for?* I hear people say. In any case, when you come to a particularly thorny passage you can ask someone else, a native speaker, to help you out." His response: "I think that position is rubbish." He even said, "My self-serving opponents point to Marcel Proust!" before retorting that "It is now widely accepted that Proust did not actually translate Ruskin," it was his mother and Marie Nordlinger who translated Ruskin.[7] (He and I move in different circles: I have never heard anyone offer that description except him.)

---

7. "The Myths and Mysteries of Literary Translation," 2020 W. G. Sebald Lecture, British Centre for Literary Translation, June 29, 2020, video, 1:30:12, https://youtu.be/GnvC8ufhnt8.

I don't think Bellos's position is rubbish, especially since
he emphasizes that the knowledge needed to translate a text
goes beyond vocabulary, syntax, and so on: using the example
of three importantly different French vocabularies for money
in Victor Hugo, he says that it's not enough to have, as it were,
sensitive antennae for moments in a text when you realize you
are missing something, because sometimes there's no signal to
pick up—what the author takes for granted he or she doesn't
explain at all, and what is not explained in the text is what
most needs to be known and understood by the translator. In
Bellos's words, "You cannot deduce from a text a code that it
doesn't explain."

That said, there are more things in heaven and earth than
are known even by an expert of Bellos's stature—there are different kinds of knowledge that a translator should have, no
one will have them all, and emphasizing some kinds goes hand
in hand with privileging or requiring a certain kind of training,
expertise, and credentialing. (David Bellos received degrees
from Oxford and is the Meredith Howland Pyne Professor of
French Literature and professor of comparative literature at
Princeton University.) At a bare minimum, what a translator
needs includes direct or indirect knowledge of the original
language (all knowledge of a dead language is indirect—Bellos
can't very well ban that!), some empathy, a desire to translate, commitment to the value of the original text and context,
skill in the language the translation will be written in, status in
the latter context, time, strength, cash, patience. Bellos may
have them all, but he takes some for granted and guards the

gates of only one or two others with his cries of Rubbish. In so doing, he mischaracterizes Proust, who couldn't speak or write English but could certainly read English—well enough to read Emerson and Thoreau in the original, for instance. His copious footnotes are filled with references to previously untranslated Ruskin passages, not supplied to him by Nordlinger or his mother, and already by 1900, before starting his translations, he claimed to know *The Seven Lamps of Architecture*, *The Bible of Amiens*, *Lectures on Architecture and Painting*, *Val d'Arno*, and Ruskin's almost six-hundred-page autobiography *Praeterita* "by heart." Bellos's description of Proust as completely incompetent and obviously incapable of translating from English is inaccurate.

In any case, Proust, not to mention other writer-translators I discuss elsewhere in this book, came to translation along different paths than Bellos did; Ruskin's books make different demands on their translator than do Victor Hugo's, Georges Perec's *Life: A User's Manual*, and the other books Bellos has translated; the intent and expectations of bringing books into Proust's French context versus Bellos's Anglo-American one were different. (Not to mention the intent and expectations, what was being asked and evaluated, in that graduate-school language exam.) It is not outrageous to demand different varieties and credentials of competence in different situations, nor to encourage translators who possess some kinds of expertise and not other kinds. I certainly know authors in other languages who read English and prefer the translations

of their work into English by (some) translators less fluent in
the original language over the translations by (some) translators more fluent in the original language—if we trust their
opinions about their own specific cases over Bellos's judgment in the abstract, then we can't call the approach rubbish. Of course, believing you don't need to know the source
language particularly well can sometimes lead to the high-
handed arrogance of people—often white, often successful,
often "Great Poets"—claiming undue credit for themselves
and erasing the work of their less prestigious collaborators,
dismissed as "native informants" or "linguists" "providing a
literal crib." So too can the other approach lead to dismiss-
ing all sorts of nonacademic modes of knowledge and experience, flattening every translation into an unimpeachable
effort to pass a language exam. There are straw men to be
found on both sides.

It seems like proper nouns should be the limiting case of this
account of language—surely a name is atomic, elemental, a
word to be considered by itself—but in fact, proper nouns
also carry meanings. Every time we write "Rome" instead of
"Roma," or "Moscow" instead of "Moskva" or "Москва," we
are translating a name, whether or not we realize it.

Uwe Johnson was a great believer in the talismanic power
of facts and names, especially as things to cling to when you
are in mourning for a life lost too soon. In *A Trip to Klagenfurt*,
his memorial book for his friend Ingeborg Bachmann written

right after her early death, he writes that Bachmann's home-
town of Klagenfurt contains Districts I–XII

with the cadastral municipalities of

Ehrental	Nagra
Blasendorf	Neudorf
Goritschen	Pubersdorf
Grossbuch	St. Martin
Grossponfeld	St. Peter
Gurlitsch I	St. Peter am Karlsberg
Hallegg	St. Peter bei Tentschach
Hörtendorf	St. Ruprecht
Klagenfurt	Stein
Kleinbuch	Tentschach
Kleinponfeld	Waidmannsdorf
Lendorf	Waltendorf
Marolla	Welzenegg

and the villages of

Amelsbichl	Gutendorf
Bach	Hallegg
Berg	Hörtendorf
Dellach	Kleinbuch
Ehrenbichl	Limmersdorf
Emmersdorf	Lippitz
Faning	Mörtschen
Görtschach	Nagra
Gottesbichl	Nessendorf
Grossbuch	Pitzelstätten

Polkeritsch	Stegendorf
Ponfeld	Schönfeld
Poppichl	Tentschach
Retschach	Trettnig
St. Jakob an der Strasse	Tultschnigg
St. Martin	Weissenbach
St. Peter am Bichl	Winklern
Seltenheim	Worounz.

He also gives the names of the forty-four political prisoners remanded into custody the day of the German annexation of Austria, as reported in the Klagenfurt newspaper. He lists the dates and times of the sixty-two Allied bombings listed in the air-defense files in Klagenfurt City Hall. These waterfalls of fact have a certain meaning—the "foreign"-sounding or Jewish-sounding names of many of those arrested; the quickening pace of the air raids as the war progressed—but they are clearly also there for their own sakes as names and dates, as monuments to reality within the wider utterance of Johnson's monument to his friend.

Yet there is also a list of thirty-five streets, lanes, and squares renamed under Nazi rule that explicitly highlights some of the ways proper nouns do carry meaning. Jews are removed: Dollfuss Square becomes Firemen Square, Dollfuss Street becomes Adolf Hitler Street, Ignaz Seipel Street becomes Palm Lane. Nazis are honored: Benedictine Square becomes S.A. Square, Main Square becomes Hermann Göring Square, Holy Ghost Square becomes Saarpfalz Square. Austrian references, even to

Austrian fascists, become German: Prince Starhemberg Street
to Nibelungs Street. Sometimes the name change is a little un-
stated history lesson, which English readers are unlikely to
grasp (Paulitsch Street to Egger Lienz Way, Kolping Avenue
to Karl Meinhardt Avenue). Sometimes it seems arbitrary,
though in this context, one wonders (Castle Street to Oak
Lane, Mill Lane to Paper Mill Lane).

One item in Johnson's list stands out: "Heinrich Heine
Avenue becomes I do not know / what it might / mean."
Heinrich Heine was a Jewish poet whose work was embedded so deep in German culture that the Nazis couldn't fully
erase him; "I do not know what it might mean" (*Ich weiß nicht,
was soll es bedeuten*) is the first line of perhaps his most classic, most classically German poem, "The Loreley." Jarringly
inserted into this list of street names—or did the Nazis *really*
rename the street with a quotation? they could have?—it expresses the willed refusal to know, to remember, your own
history or even geography, what all the streets you walk down
used to be called. When I translated *A Trip to Klagenfurt* into
English, I left as is even the translatable parts of the list of villages and cadastral municipalities (such as their prepositions—
"on the Karlsberg," "near Tentschach"), because the meanings
of those names mattered less than the waterfall of concrete
facts; for this list, though, it was important to get as much as
possible into English: "Street," "Lane," translating *Marktplatz,
Heiligengeistplatz, Feuerwehrplatz* as "Market Square," "Holy
Ghost Square," "Firemen Square." Otherwise Johnson's literary effects would be lost.

Other texts, other names blend foreign fact with translatable meaning in other ways and have to be handled differently. Fredrikstadbrua in Norway is like a gray-scale palette of name versus meaning: in English you can set the transition wherever you want, calling it Fredrikstadbrua or Fredrikstad Bridge or Fredrik City Bridge or Frederick City Bridge (the city is named after the king known in English as King Frederick II), or Fredericksburg Bridge, for that matter.

There is also the question of familiarity. I have translated "Burgtor" as "Burgtor Gate," even though this is a pleonasm— "*Tor*" means "Gate." (Pleonasm: a rhetorical term meaning the use of redundant words, saying the same thing more than once—e.g., "burning flame," "completely impossible," "PIN number.") What went into this decision was that (1) German readers would know that the Burgtor is a famous medieval city gate in Lübeck, and the translation conveys in English what the reader needs to know; (2) I assume that some readers have seen or heard of the Burgtor while others won't know what it is; (3) "Burgtor Gate," to my ear, intangibly conveys a German place-name better than "Burg Gate," which would be too strange a yoking of languages, or "City Gate" as the proper name for the city gate, which doesn't add much of anything. On the other hand, I can't imagine a situation where I would translate Paris's Gare du Nord as "North Station" or "Gare du Nord Station," because I assume that English-language readers have a greater familiarity with those French words than with "*Tor*" (or "*brua*"), so the meaning is more or less clear. If needed, I could always add clarification: "the train arriving at

Gare du Nord" or "Gare du Nord in a northern arrondissement
of the city." I would be more inclined to translate Kaiserstrasse
as Kaiser Street than as Kaiserstrasse Street, and in any case
it's unlikely to become Emperor Avenue, unless the imperial aspect is given great symbolic weight in a particular text,
while Keizersgracht in Amsterdam would more likely stay in
Dutch or become Keizersgracht Canal, like Burgtor Gate, or
else go all the way to Emperor's Canal. This is logically in-
consistent because what determines the decision are factors
besides logic: how much meaning and how much foreignness
Kaiser or Keizer or Burg conveys on its own; how familiar I
imagine *-strasse* or *-tor* or *-gracht* to be; how famous the places
themselves are (Keizersgracht is a major tourist attraction in
Amsterdam, while Kaiserstrasse just a nice boulevard in Mainz
or a short street in Berlin). And if a character in a novel travels
from Mainz to Amsterdam, I might want to override one of
these separate decisions and handle the two place-names the
same way in the same book.

People's names have the same blend as well—there is no
universal principle. It might seem that we should always preserve what people call themselves, but of course we don't:
not only are there transliterations, and old anglicizations that
are now generally accepted ("Scheherezade"), or accepted in
some contexts ("Peking duck" despite "Beijing"), there are
also translations. I grew up with Native American names often
being translations, not just for Sitting Bull or Crazy Horse: I was
told that "Indian names always mean something"—He-Who-
Follows-Winding-Paths-through-the-Forest or whatever. This

was both a form of respectful communication—giving readers information they don't have, like the meaning of "*Tor*"—and a way of dismissively exoticizing Native Americans as close to nature, totemic, or what have you. We don't say that the famous singer who died young of anorexia was Karen She-Who-Builds-with-Wood, or that the most common name in English is John He-Who-Forges-in-Metal. It's hard to imagine a situation where a common Japanese name like Yamada (山田) or Yukiko (雪子) would be "translated"—they mean "Mountain field" and "Little snow" or "Little snow child," respectively—because Japanese people don't experience the names that way in regular life, any more than English Carpenters or Smiths do. (Borderline case: the names Rose and Violet and Lily do flickeringly register as flowers, and I can imagine these being translated.) But while there are some situations where referring to Sitting Bull by his Lakota name, Tȟatȟáŋka Íyotake, would be more appropriate, there are others where it would not be. Do speakers of Lakota think about Sitting with the Buffalo when they hear "Tȟatȟáŋka Íyotake"? And is that the relevant question? Or is it really about how comfortable English readers in a given context can be assumed to be with the name "Tȟatȟáŋka," including all those unfamiliar accents and characters, as opposed to "Yamada." Sometimes, removing the accents or academic spelling is taken to be enough (Shakyamuni, Muhammad, *terma* instead of Śākyamuni, Muḥammad, *gterma*). This arguably makes more sense when transliterating from a different alphabet anyway (शाक्यमुनि, مُحَمَّد, གཏེར་མ་), though the Croatian writer Dubravka Ugrešić, coming from the

same Latin alphabet as ours, chose to spell her name "Ugresic"
in English-language publications (and German, French, etc.),
even though this spelling changes the Croatian pronunciation
from "Ugreshitch" to "Ugresick." Lakota didn't have a written
alphabet at all until the mid-nineteenth century, so all those
accents and symbols truly are English-language decisions, and
we too must decide: are we writing a name for linguists or
for communication with general readers? "Tatángka" Íyotake
would work better than "Tȟatȟáŋka" in many contexts, such
as history textbooks.

There are no rules, only decisions. (Unlike Ugrešić, the
writer Saša Stanišić feels confident or stubborn enough,
for whatever reason, whether gender or age or personality
or writing in German or something else, to keep those same
accents on his name in German and English.) And all of these
issues come into play in a translation, along with accidents of
sound and crosslinguistic coincidence. Jon Fosse's *Septology*
has one of the great dog characters in literature: a little guy
who curls up with the narrator under his blanket, goes outside to run in circles in the snow and take a piss, is constantly
falling off the narrator's lap when the narrator forgets about
him and stands up, and occasionally looks up at the narrator with his dog eyes and it's like they understand everything,
like nothing is hidden from them, but there's no way he can
ever say it in words. More than one reader has told me that
this dog is their favorite character in the books. In Norwegian,
the dog's name is Brage (pronounced *BROG-eh*), and that is
how I kept it through all my draft translations of the first book

until at some point it clicked in my mind that English speakers would likely hear this in their heads as rhyming with "rage"
and "page." Brage-rhymes-with-rage is not a good dog name,
and now that I was thinking about it, even Brogguh is less cute
in English than it is in Norwegian, it sounds kind of heavy. I
asked Fosse if the name meant anything special to him and he
reminded me that Brage is the Norse god of poetry—I hadn't
recognized it because the name I had always seen in books of
Norse myths was "Bragi," the Old Norse and Icelandic spelling. This made the dog's name even better, like if you named
your silly little shih tzu "Apollo" or "Orpheus." Calling the dog
"Bragi" would make readers like me more likely to pick up on
that. Plus, it sounds cute, and even, I later realized, subliminally
rhymes with "doggie" (in my pronunciation of English). I will
never know for sure, but I am convinced that English-language
readers would not have loved Brage as much as they love Bragi
and that changing the name was one of the best translation decisions I made in those books.

What counts as a word? You have probably heard the line that
"Eskimo languages have thirty-two words for snow" (or fifty,
or a hundred). I am not alone in finding this cliché irritating.
The fact is, English has hundreds of kinds of snow too: "new
snow," "wet snow," "blinding snow in the sunlight," "snow
perfect for making snowballs with," "disgusting four-month-
old mounds of black snow around the edges of the parking
lot" . . . These phrases each use more than one word, but who
cares? Adjectives in English are separate words or phrases

from their nouns, not joined in a compound, but this is a minor technicality, not a sign of one culture's deeper insight into weather conditions than another's.[8] It would be like saying Norwegians have "a hundred words for bridge" "because bridges are so important in their culture": Fredrikstadbrua, Brooklynbrua, Londonbrua . . .

The fact that units of meaning are counted differently in different languages also has consequences for the issue of repetition of the same word within a given text—for it is neither universal nor obvious what counts as the "same" word in a language. English has quite a low tolerance for exact repetition; it is expected in good writing that replication be avoided in favor of synonyms—so-called "elegant variation"—or else that the whole passage be rewritten and streamlined. (In the previous sentence I used "repetition" and "replication," "synonyms" and "variation," "good" and "elegant," rather than any doubles except "in" and "that" and "be.") I say exact repetition, but a sentence with both "synonym" and "synonyms," or both "varies" and "varied," would likewise be felt to be inelegant despite the words not matching exactly. There are only a couple of well-defined exceptions to the ban on repetition in English, such as dialogue tags, where the simple, functional "he said" and "she said" are customary, while reaching for "he exclaimed," "she urged," "he queried," "she pontificated"

8. The English-language *Farmer's Almanac*, incidentally, lists forty different terms for snow that aren't adjectival phrases, from "barchan" through "powder" to "whiteout," with only fifteen of them being compounds including "snow" (https://www.farmersalmanac.com/how-many-words-snow).

is generally considered a rather shoddy trick to get around making the dialogue speak for itself. Because repetition is relatively rare in English except in such situations, it is significant—it stands out thematically or symbolically when two things or characters are described as being the same adjective or doing the same verb.

But this threshold is different in different languages. Verbs are often generic in German and repeated more often than in English, without their repetition being especially significant. Dawn, mentioned twenty times in Homer's *Odyssey*, is evoked with the same line every time: "But when early-born rosy-fingered Dawn appeared . . ."[9] In a sense, the whole line is a single unit of meaning, a single "word"—"rosy-fingered" isn't a transportable adjective that is ever applied to another figure, nor can Dawn do anything but appear, or have any other body parts, or have fingers that are anything but rosy. However, few readers would find the exact same line all twenty times acceptable in English. Wilson chooses to vary her translations, creating a little firecracker of excitement for the English reader each time we come across another variation and get to see her new but always perfectly iambic sunrise. There are obvious enough reasons for repeating Homeric epithets, related to the originally oral storytelling of Homer's epics; my point isn't that they're acceptable in English or not—it's that it doesn't make sense to talk about units being repeated independent of the conventions of the language those repetitions are in.

9. Wilson, introduction to *Odyssey*, p. 5.

Which means that to justify using the same repetitions you need to argue that repetition functions the same way in both languages—that the repetitions deviate from the baseline in the same way. Marian Schwartz's 2014 retranslation of *Anna Karenina* presented itself as the first to "embrace Tolstoy's unusual style" in English, refusing to "clean up" his "supposed mistakes and infelicities" and, especially, choosing to use repetition in English to match his "signature repetitions" in Russian. Her translation of the novel's second paragraph begins:

> The Oblonsky home was all confusion. The wife had found out about her husband's affair with the French governess formerly in their home and had informed her husband that she could not go on living in the same house with him. This had been the state of affairs for three days now, and it was keenly felt not only by the spouses themselves but by all the members of the family and the servants as well. All the members of the family and the servants felt that there was no sense in their living together and that travelers chancing to meet in any inn had more in common than did they, the Oblonsky family members and servants.

The rest of the paragraph adds yet another "home" and "house," plus "housekeeper," "rooms," and "premises," to the two "home"s and one "house" in the first two sentences and the family members and servants three times in two more sentences. Schwartz's translator's note calls out this passage in particular, with its "bludgeoning" repetitions, before insisting that these are not mistakes but rather an intentional device. No other English translators have followed the Russian repetitions so closely, but Schwartz translated the book "in the firm belief that Tolstoy wholly intended to bend language to his will, as an instrument of his aesthetic and moral convictions."[10] This is clearly true, but the question is whether or not the English language bends differently.

Schwartz's judgment is that Tolstoy's prose is *unusually* repetitive in Russian, unlike Homer's epithets for Dawn in Greek, and so her translation in English should be too. This may well be true, but Milan Kundera, who as a bilingual novelist should have known better, falsely made the point universal: using French translations of Kafka to criticize translators in general, he labels the decision to use fewer repetitions "the *synonymizing reflex*—a reflex of nearly all translators." While it "seems innocent," Kundera says, its "systematic quality inevitably smudges the original idea. And besides, what the hell for? Why not say 'go' when the author says *'gehen'*?" Well, German uses *gehen* differently than how English can use *go*, that's why. German uses verbs differently than English *tout court*. Kundera wants strict word-for-word replication, denying that languages repeat differently.[11]

---

10. Schwartz, in Leo Tolstoy, *Anna Karenina*, (Yale University Press, 2014), p. xxiii.

11. *Testaments Betrayed: An Essay in Nine Parts*, tr. Linda Asher (Harper Perennial, 1995), p. 108; in Kundera's original French, the reprehensible translation is of the German *gehen* as *marcher* (walk) instead of *aller* (go). Kundera follows

The point is worth lingering on: parts of speech, along with word boundaries and what counts as repeated words, are not fixed truths that are the same across different languages. In German or French you say, "I have hunger"; in English, "I'm hungry." Everyone knows not to translate *Ich habe Hunger* or *J'ai faim* as "I have hunger," but not everyone generalizes from there to the fact that parts of speech function differently in different languages. A German-English dictionary will tell you that something is a noun, but not that nouns work differently in English and German.

German nouns can unproblematically be abstract and are often used as the subject of active verbs, whereas English wants adjectives and concrete, animate subjects: in German one might say, without being over the top, "a large fear rose up

---

the passage quoted above with a homophobic slur, riffing on his term "synonymizing": "O ye translators, do not sodonymize us!"

As Polizzotti writes in his discussion of this passage (*Sympathy for the Traitor*, pp. 14–15), "In English there might be moments when *go* works better, others when Joseph K. should *leave*, and still others when he's got to *move*." This argument, while enough to refute Kundera's stupid claim, is quite a bit narrower than my argument: I say that even when *gehen* does mean *go*, languages use verbs and repetition and simplicity differently overall, so there are not just semantic reasons to vary the translation. Strangely, this seems to be Kundera's wider point—that repetition has a melody, a literary importance, and needs to be attended to in translation—but he then imposes a universal rule that ignores his own argument. Not quite universal, though. He grants that there is "one single word that does not support a word-for-word translation" in the passage he discusses: "*fremd*." Kafka's metaphor of a man in love feeling "*in der Fremde*" can't be translated "*à l'étranger*" (abroad, in another country) but should instead be "*dans un monde étranger*" (in a strange world): in this case, the use of a "paraphrase" with two French words—he doesn't grant it the status of a translation—"seems comprehensible" to him (*Les Testaments trahis* [Gallimard, 1993], pp. 125–128, my translations).

within me," which in English means "I felt scared" or "I started to get very scared" (because I am a subject who feels; scared is an emotion a person feels; fear isn't something inside a person like a tumor, and big or small, and rising up or moving around in any other way under its own power). While German nouns are vigorous and interesting, usually compounded together with built-in prepositional spatiality, the verbs, as I've mentioned, are often generic: *stehen, stellen, machen, haben,* Kundera's old favorite *gehen* ("stand," "put," "make" or "do," "have," "go"), and their numerous compounds. In English, though, the verbs are where the action is; nouns without enlivening adjectives or verbs are static.[12] A good translation from German has to denounify: Uwe Johnson wittily describes an office building's elevator giving a little downward stutter before it rises, saying the cabin *"geht in die Knie"* ("goes down on one knee" or "kneels on both knees"); Kundera would presumably insist that we have to keep *gehen* as "go" and write that this personified elevator cabin "goes into the knee," but in English it "genuflects."[13] A Thomas Mann character at one

12. The editor Edwin Frank first made this point about German nouns and verbs to me, in the context of revising my translated sentences to be better English. I continued to think about and expand on the argument implied by his point, but the insight is thanks to him.

13. Likewise translations from Spanish: "English does great verbs: I just took a phrase which in Spanish was something like 'I pulled up with great and abrupt strength' and translated it as 'I yanked'" (Daniel Hahn, *Catching "Fire": A Translation Diary* [Charco, 2022], p. 128). As for French, Jacques Barzun writes that "it prefers verbs that are as neutral as possible and it throws the emphasis on the noun. Thus: not 'frighten' but *faire peur*; not 'kick' but *donner un coup de pied*; not 'compete' but *entrer en concurrence*; not 'cry out' but *pousser des cris*; and so on."

point says, "The independence and self-sufficiency of my imagination was additionally delightful," using three nouns, two of them expressing an intangible quality or feeling, plus an inelegant -*ly* adverb; fully in English, what he means is that "relying entirely on my imagination was even more enjoyable" (one noun). In tighter American English: "just making stuff up is even better." But the narrator here, Felix Krull, is wordy and roundabout, so that phrasing wouldn't work in his voice.

This Mann example is in a way typical of the translation process. Just as I called "Fredrikstadbrua" a gray-scale palette where you can draw the line between what to put in English and what to leave in Norwegian anywhere in the word, what I just described feels a bit like turning an old analog radio dial up and down toward German sounding and English sounding, trying to find the precise frequency of the station you want. The version that uses actual German words is out of range, but between the literal translation preserving the parts of speech at one end of the dial—"the independence and self-sufficiency of my imagination was additionally delightful"— and the all-American colloquialism at the other end, I slide

---

While French, like German, makes verbs and adjectives into nouns (*le savior, un boire, une pauvre, la bonne*), "English works the other way and makes nouns into verbs and adjectives: we *sun* ourselves, the laundry *irons* the shirts; a *music* critic, the *French* concert, and so on" (*An Essay on French Verse: For Readers of English Poetry* [New Directions, 1991], p. 14). (The French language patterns, in this case the ability of French, like German, to naturally use impersonal subjects with action verbs, may have tripped Barzun up slightly here: to my ear, "the laundry irons the shirts" sounds slightly off—I feel English pushes us to say "at the laundry they iron the shirts," or else if I was making up an example I would say "the valet irons the shirt.")

the translation back and forth in ever smaller increments, to home in on what sounds right for this moment of this particular text. Another example of this process is the case of the repeated catchphrase in André Gide's *Marshlands*—"*Tiens! Tu travailles?*"—previously translated into campy British English as "I say! Are you writing?"; retranslated by me as "So! Hard at work?"; and justified as not too extreme or anachronistic an Americanism by comparison with the truly colloquial "Hey. Busy?"[14]

In any case, the German reliance on nouns is why translations of German philosophy can be so turgid: complicated nouns with bland or impersonal verbs don't capture in English the precision and intensity of the German, they clog it up and slow it down. You don't want to say that an object "has a usefulness-nature that allows it to be . . . ," you want to

14. Gide, *Marshlands* (New York Review Book Classics, 2021), p. xix.

As a strategy, some translators say it's a good idea to have the extreme over-translation in mind before you try to pinpoint the sweet spot you want. Harry Mathews gives this advice in his great essay "Translation and the Oulipo": "When I translate, I begin by studying the original text until I understand it thoroughly. Then, knowing that I can *say* anything I understand, no matter how awkwardly, I say what I have now understood and write down my words. I imagine myself talking to a friend across the table to make sure the words I use are ones I naturally speak. . . . Translating the opening sentence of Proust—*Longtemps je me suis couché de bonne heure* [For a long time I used to go to bed early]—I might write down: When I was a kid, it took me years to get my parents to let me even stay up till *nine*. . . . There is still work to do. But I have gained an enormous advantage. . . . Instead of having to move *away* from the foreign text, I can now move *towards* it as I improve my clumsy rendering, sure that at every step, with the source text as my goal, I shall be working in native English" (in *The Case of the Persevering Maltese: Collected Essays* [Dalkey Archive, 2003], pp. 77–78, originally published in *Brick* 57 [Fall 1997]: 39–44).

say, "people use it to . . . ," with a human subject and active
main verb ("person acts," not "thing has a quality"). When
a writer like Marx deploys his complicated neologistic compound nouns—"The money-form of the commodity confronts the commodity-form of the worker's labor" or what
have you—it has life and a playful, exciting energy in German,
from the nouns; the generic verb *stehen* plus preposition (*steht
gegenüber*, "confronts" or "stands facing"), which Marx repeats
over and over again in *Capital,* produces in German a kind
of quivering equilibrium between these energies. In English
it sounds like the world's worst cocktail party: all these stiff
creatures standing around not talking to one another. But the
temptation among academic philosophy translators is to be
extraliteral about the nouns, especially in crucial moments of
the German, precisely where the English most needs verbal
energy.

Titles pose special problems of translation, since at first
sight there is no context of other passages to fill in what a
given translation choice leaves out; the title has crucial functions of describing and signaling and advertising, above and
beyond the words of the rest of the text. When I translated
Saša Stanišić's autobiographical novel, called *Herkunft* in German, as *Where You Come From,* several readers and reviewers
pointed out that *Herkunft* means "origin" or "origins," sometimes "provenance," "ancestry," ethnic or national "background." Why did I, as they put it, change the title? For one
thing, because *Origin* would be a terrible title for a novel. A
title like Alex Haley's *Roots* works well because his theme is

rootedness, and English nouns are rooted. One's "roots" are in a unique place, and being dug up and transplanted can be fatal or at least disorienting and harmful. That's what Haley's book is about. Stanišić's *Herkunft* is about how everyone starts someplace or another—the first accident of life, Stanišić says, is where you happen to be born—and we make something from that starting place, something that often involves moving, emigrating, immigrating, exile, finding and creating new homes. *Herkunft* doesn't have noun-in-English energy, dug into the soil: it is the start of a dynamic process.

In principle, a noun title in German needn't be a noun in English, but what about *Herkunft* in particular? Like many German nouns, it's a dynamic compound: *her* is a preposition meaning "from someplace else toward here." (Together with "where," or *wo* in German, "*Woher kommt sie*" means "Where does she come from"; "*Wohin geht sie*" means "Where is she going [to].") The second half of the word, -*kunft*, is derived from the verb *kommen*, "to come (toward)," and suggests the finished product of that verbal act. It appears in many German compounds with prepositions: a plane or train's "arrival" is its *Ankunft* (coming to its destination, *an* means "at" or "to"); the future is the *Zukunft* (coming at us, *zu* means "toward"); information, especially information you've asked someone for, is *Auskunft* (what comes out, *aus* means "out"). *Herkunft*, then, is the someplace-else at the start of the journey-that-brought-you-here. "Where You Come From" is actually a *more* literal translation than "Origin," as well as working better and sounding better.

The only thing added in the English is the pronoun, because verbs in English generally need subjects and you can't say "Where Come From." Since *Herkunft* is by a living author, I could at this point simply send him an email and ask him whether he wanted his book to be called *Where I Come From*, emphasizing his own unique personal journey, or *Where You Come From*, emphasizing that everyone has their own comparable situation of having started at a given point. I mentioned in the email that the word "You" here is an impersonal third-person pronoun, because we don't naturally say "Where One Comes From" anymore, but it still has a little second-person energy, drawing the reader into thinking about his or her own personal starting point. Stanišić went with option B, and I agreed, and there's the title.

While one German word became four words in English, we have already seen that the boundaries of words—the "units" of meaning—depend on the language. "*Herkunft*" should really be thought of as two units, not one: "whither" plus "come." "Whither" has turned into "from where" in contemporary English, and "come" requires a subject, so "Where You Come From" has the same units of meaning as "*Herkunft*," and a different number of words only in the most trivial, mechanical sense.

Just as parts of speech often need to be adjusted to the conventions of the translating language, negatives too can be especially interesting moments in translation, because different languages have units with different valences. In some languages, "she never does" things; in others, "no one ever does" them. "They had never," "They hadn't ever," "No one had ever," "Everyone had always not": these are natural or not in different ways in different languages. In other words, the baseline in a given language might be the positive or negative form, the individual or collective formulation, and so you often need to translate negatives as positives or vice versa; the reversals in a sentence need to come in the right places. In Norwegian, there are a lot of times in conversations when people stop and look at each other, or just look down, and *"det vert stilt."* It is awkward to translate this phrase as "it got quiet" or "they fell silent" or "a silence fell" (or "descended") or "there was a pause," although these are all dictionary definitions of *det vert stilt*. More natural translations into English use a negative, either as subject, verb, or object: "no one said anything," "they didn't speak a word," "they said nothing for a moment." Norwegian has these too: *ikkje seia noko*, "not say anything"; *dei seier ikkje noko*, "they said nothing." But those aren't quite how you'd naturally say it in Norwegian. Just as you shouldn't translate the normal Norwegian literally, ignoring the conventions of positive/negative in English, you shouldn't do the same in the other direction.

As I mention in discussing "not this but that," German embodies a different set of assumptions about conflict and agreement, denial and assertion than English, and these assumptions, these baseline conventions, interact with the use of negation as well. There is an active German verb for keeping quiet: *schweigen*, "to not-talk"; *er schweigt*, "he not-talked." This gives being silent a somewhat different level of intentionality and choice than in English, where being silent is typically an absence of action, not an action in its own right: in German, *schweigen* is active, so an inanimate object can't *schweigen*—only a person, stealthy animal, or other living force such as "Nature" or "the forest," which could in theory make a sound, can *schweigen*. In English, though, dead things or empty spaces can "be silent"—outer space, a rock, an abandoned alleyway, spring with all the animals extinct. A good translation of *schweigen* into English often has to add a negative and/or use an active verb to express the intentionality of keeping silent: "she said nothing," "he chose not to respond," "she decided to keep her mouth shut."

The fact that we translate utterances, not words, also means that no words are untranslatable. I was giving a talk once with a writer I'd translated, and he was telling the audience one of those stories about untranslatable words—you know the kind—in this case a word from an indigenous language in southern Patagonia, and the word means, well, when a man and a woman are in a bar, and he looks at her, and she looks at him, and they look at each other and their looks say okay I'm interested in you but you need to make the first move and come over to me? The word means that. Everyone laughed, the writer is charming and tells a good story. He'd told the story because I had just said that as a translator I didn't like to admit anything was untranslatable. Now I said, "See, you

translated it! You told us in English, and everybody laughed!"
He said, "But you can't translate it in one word—" and I said,
"Well, what matters more to you, how many words it has or
whether everybody laughs?"[15]

Translators read to decide what's important and what's
less important, then re-create what they've decided is important; the debates about whether to translate literally or for
the overall sense, whether to domesticate a term or leave it
foreign sounding, whether to translate rhymed and metered

---

15. The writer was the Austrian playwright Clemens Berger; the word, which
is a cliché of untranslatability, was *mamihlapinatapai*, from Yagán, an indigenous
language of Tierra del Fuego. Perhaps you are wondering why this particular
word, and not any number of others, gained its pride of place on all those in-
ternet lists of untranslatable words? Like most clichés, this one too started as a
contingent possibility among others in a specific context. The classicist Jane Ellen Harrison was a member of the Cambridge Ritualists, a group of scholars who
brought modern theories of "primitive" ritual into the study of ancient Greece;
in her view of language, the "savages" lived without our modern-day separation
between subject and object, self and world. "Language, after the purely emotional
interjection, began with whole sentences, *holophrases*, utterances of a relation in
which subject and object have not yet got their heads above water, but are still
submerged in a situation." Harrison called this holistic merging of self and world
a *holopsychosis* and gave as an example, complete with a hint of partly unspoken
holosexual subtext, "the Fuegians have a word or rather holophrase *mamihlapinatapai* which means 'looking-at-each-other,-hoping-that-either-will-offer-to-do-
something-which-both-parties-desire-but-are-unwilling-to-do.' This holophrase
is quite unanalysable, it contains no nouns and no verbs, it simply expresses an intense relation not unknown to some of us." Harrison's linguistics here is nonsense:
the word is perfectly analyzable, into the reflexive/passive prefix *ma-* (*mam-* before a vowel); the root *ihlapi*, meaning "to be at a loss as what to do next"; the
stative suffix *-n*; an achievement suffix, *-ata*; and the dual suffix *-apai*, which
gives the reflexive *mam-* a reciprocal sense. But the feeling of being intensely
submerged in a situation was no doubt real, and Harrison's choice of desire waiting painfully for someone else to make the first move as an example to illustrate

poetry with rhyme and meter, and all the rest are pointless, because—obviously—it depends. These decisions tend to get made unconsciously and instinctively, even if the translator likes to rationalize them afterward, and the decisions are different in every novel or story or poem or instruction manual, and at every moment of every such utterance. Now what matters is a rhyme, a joke, a repetition, a specific description of a particular object, a verbal tic, verve, historical accuracy, sentence structure, now it's something else—in instruction manuals it's mostly the literal content—and translators snake

---

the intense bond of "holopsychosis" was no accident. In the year this romanticizing primitivism was published, Harrison was living in Paris with her nearly forty years younger ex-student and life companion, Hope Mirrlees, thirty-one at the time, who was writing a lost modernist classic called *Paris: A Poem*, which was published the next year, in 1920, by the Hogarth Press, owned by Leonard and Virginia Woolf; the whole poem is a coded lesbian love letter propelled by a desire for fluid, collective experience, and its first line is "I want a holophrase." Virginia Woolf appreciated the text of *Paris* and surely its subtext; she hand-corrected the manuscript and typeset the poem herself for Hogarth, calling it "obscure, indecent, and brilliant." It and Mirrlees fell into deeper obscurity, but *mamihlapinatapai* had entered into circulation in English, and here we are. Jane Ellen Harrison, *Aspects, Aorists and the Classical Tripos* (Cambridge University Press, 1919), p. 16. Her book too is interesting as a coded love letter; its opening lines are: "Twice in my life, only twice, it has happened to me to fall in love with a language. Once, long ago, with Greek, again, only yesterday as it seems to me, with Russian. To fall in love with a language is an enchanting experience. You feel as though you were born again, you wonder how you could ever have lived without your new love; life seems growing richer every moment." On the holophrase, she cites p. 473 of her own book *Themis: A Study of the Social Origins of Greek Religion* (Cambridge University Press, 1912) and gives as her ethnographic source "Mr E. J. Payne's sections on language in his *History of the New World*, 1899, vol. II, p. 114 ff." On Mirrlees and *Paris*, see Dustin Illingworth's 2021 essay "Little Funny Things Ceaselessly Happening," https://www.poetryfoundation.org/articles/155427/little-funny -things-ceaselessly-happening.

through the text carving off what they can live without from what they can't. They gerrymander unscrupulously. Because if what matters is that look in a bar, then the translator needs to spend a sentence or two describing it, or include a footnote (a footnote isn't "added to" the translation, it's part of the translation).[16] If what matters is keeping the text smooth and lively with no footnotes, then that's what you're translating for and that's what you'll get. If a character says something that would take fifteen words or inappropriately technical language to express in English so you substitute something else to keep the conversation moving, that doesn't mean the word for that thing was untranslatable—it means that you're translating for naturalness of dialogue. Anything left untranslated is what you've decided doesn't matter anyway.

In a deeper sense, nothing *can be* left untranslated. Since translation is realignment, nothing will stay fixed—nothing can stay fixed, even if you want it to. When you look at the world from a different location, aiming your gaze in a different direction, every angle and occlusion and vector will change. To say something is untranslatable is to say that every reader in all of space and time would read it the same way, and that is

16. Most publishers nowadays, especially university presses, prefer endnotes to footnotes, partly because they are much easier to format for ebooks. I had to fight to get footnotes in the present book, rather than endnotes, because I feel they work differently: they create a kind of stereoscopic form of address as opposed to providing reference material that readers can look up in the back of the book. They change how the text functions—they are part of how the book is written—so the decision whether and how to use them will be part of any translation strategy.

not what reading is. (It would be like saying a chair is always seen from the same angle.) The limiting case is described in Borges's amazing story of Pierre Menard, who tried to write a book that would be word for word the same as *Don Quixote*. Once he succeeded, for a couple of chapters, the result was a different book despite every last word being exactly the same. It was different because realigned: *Don Quixote* written by a French Symbolist poet for modern readers.

A class of examples that makes the impossibility of untranslatability especially clear is when a word or passage is in a foreign language in the original text. Even if you leave it in the other language, you can't leave it untranslated. For example, Tolstoy's novels have a lot of dialogue in French: the characters' use of French was meaningful information, and he also expected his readers to know French. Some of Tolstoy's translators into English keep the French and put a translation in a footnote or endnote; some translate the French, with or without slipping in "he said in French" instead of "he said." Since twenty-first-century American readers cannot be expected to have the same relationship to French as Tolstoy's nineteenth-century Russian readers, simply keeping the French without a note is not automatically the right translation choice. And even if that is the choice a translator makes, those French utterances have been realigned—translated into things characters say in an English-language book. They are as different from Tolstoy's original French dialogue as Menard's words are from Cervantes's.

A student of mine once wrestled with the problem of a Greek short story whose title was in an Albanian-influenced dialect, mostly but not entirely unintelligible to Greek readers, that also comes up at several key moments in the story itself. He was tempted to leave the words untranslated in the title and either translate them in a footnote later or explain them in a headnote earlier; I pointed out that since such a headnote or footnote would in fact be translating the words of the title, why not put English words into the title itself and put the explanation of the other language in the note? Do you want something fully incomprehensible as your title? Whatever you do, you're translating puzzling text in the original into puzzling text in the translation, and your job is to make sure it functions in the analogous way that works best in English.

Several books I have translated use English foreign words—that is, English words in the German or French original book. This is clearly a special case of the situation we saw with Tolstoy's use of French: the English-language reader's relationship to English cannot possibly be the same as the original reader's; the relationship between the English phrase and the rest of the text cannot be the same when the rest of the text is also in English. When the author chooses English, because the dialogue is spoken by Americans or because he or she she wants to call attention to an ideological implication or other quirk of the English language, I have often indicated that to the reader, for example with a note in the front of the book: "All text in SMALL CAPS is in English in the original."

When the author's ear for English isn't perfect and he or she has a character say something they would never actually say, for instance a New York cabdriver saying "Madam" instead of "Ma'am," I translate the author's English-language dialogue into English: the taxi driver who in the German original says "Yes madam" now says "YES, MA'AM." There is nothing to be gained by incorporating a gotcha on the original author's competence in English. Sometimes, when I feel that the English language has just permeated the other language and the author is using English words ("laptop," "sweet sixteen") alongside his or her other vocabulary, not making any point *about* English, it works to simply leave those words unmarked in the translation. In effect, the word is just a cognate, indistinguishable from all the other German or French words of the original.

Uwe Johnson's *Anniversaries* does all these things and more. The French and Czech and Russian in the book can be left as is (or, more precisely: translated in the English version with the same unannotated French or Czech or Russian words), because Johnson doesn't assume his original reader necessarily understands them either: he explains the necessary context in the text himself or leaves it as incomprehensible linguistic texture. On the other hand, the characters' thoughts and memories in Plattdeutsch, a regional dialect of German, can't be left as is, because they are sort of in German, semi-intelligible to Johnson's general German readers but fully (or largely) unintelligible to English-language readers. So I made up vaguely dialecty spellings and put those sentences in italics, to indicate linguistic difference without making those passages too alien: "*Go on an call em mountains. Even if theyre Mecklenburg mountains.*" When the German mother and American daughter characters have bilingual conversations about differences between English and German, still other strategies and explanations are necessary.

Finally, since an utterance can contain words of other languages, or Bakhtinian voices in intonations inflected by other languages, we might say that no language is truly monolingual. This is true in a far more general sense than the superficial case of quoting dialogue in other languages. Take what I described above as a German tic: the not-this-but-that construction. Uwe Johnson's favorite writer, who influenced him in many ways, was William Faulkner, and Faulkner's later novels with their long clawing grasping searching sentences prominently use this same move of negation and correction. Here are a very few examples from the early pages of *The Wild Palms* (1939):

> It was a beach cottage, even though of two stories, and lighted by oil lamps—or an oil lamp. . . . And the doctor wore a night shirt too, not pajamas.

> It was after midnight, though not much. He could tell that, even apart from the wind.

> So he graduated, nearer the foot of the class than the head though not at either.

[She] sat all day long in a new cheap beach chair facing the
water . . . , not reading, not doing anything, just sitting there
in that complete immobility which the doctor (or the doctor
in the Doctor) did not need [corroboration] to recognise at
once—that complete immobile abstraction from which even
pain and terror are absent. [A bit later he walks past her in the
beach chair] with no sign from her, no movement of the head
or perhaps even of the eyes.[17]

So are such constructions in Johnson's novel deliberate
Faulknerisms? Johnson wasn't the "completely separated
person" that Schleiermacher imagines. His German has
some Faulkner in it, and of course *Anniversaries* is set in New
York, thus much of what it describes in German, even the
dialogue, supposedly happened in English. Does that mean
we need to try to make Johnson's sentences in English sound
like Faulkner? Meanwhile, Faulkner had found his searching, circling prose strategies in Joseph Conrad—*Lord Jim*
absolutely reads like Faulkner, or was able to be read like
Faulkner once Faulkner came along. Then, English was Conrad's third language, so maybe Conrad's English bears traces
of Polish conventions? And so on. What language is Johnson's tic now?

A useful teaching exercise I've tried on occasion is to ask
everyone in a class to raise their hand if they know more than

17. Quoted from the edition *If I Forget Thee, Jerusalem* (Vintage International,
1995), pp. 3–5.

one language, then tell the students who didn't raise their
hands that "you're bilingual too," because of the split Lati-
nate/Germanic vocabulary of the English language and its
roots in history. They already know the difference between
"Help!" and "I request assistance," between a ceremony formal enough to be called "commencement" and a "fresh start";
they can appreciate why science sounds intellectual in English
because of words imported during the Renaissance, like *sul-
fur, hypotenuse, marine biology*, as opposed to if these were
called "stinkstone" or "longline" or "sea lore"; they can quickly
grasp the political history of these different registers going
back to the Norman Conquest (on the Anglo-Saxon peasant's
farm, it's *cow, lamb, pig*; on the French nobleman's table, it's
beef, mutton, pork; the words *estate* and *property* are Latinate,
while the *rent* that's due is Anglo-Saxon). I hand out two passages from Chaucer's prologue to *The Canterbury Tales*—the
first lines describing the fancy Maunciple and the first lines
describing the ruddy Shipman—and the students can map the
different etymologies to see something about the multiplicity
of English, even pre-Renaissance English, and how Chaucer
uses it to create characters:

> A gentil MAUNCIPLE was there of a temple,
> Of which achatours myghte take exemple
> For to be wise in byynge [buying] of vitaille;
> For wheither that he payde or took by taille,
> Algate he wayted so in his achaat
> That he was ay biforn and in good staat. . . .

A SHIPMAN was ther, wonynge fer by weste;

For aught I woot, he was of Dertemouthe.

He rood upon a rouncy, as he kouthe [as best he could],

In a gowne of faldyng to the knee.

A daggere hangynge on a laas hadde he

About his nekke, under his arm adoun. . . .

"Maunciple" and "gentil" are from French, along with "acha-tours" and "achaat" (cf. *acheter*), "vitaille" (provisions), and "by taille" (on credit); the Anglo-Saxon "shipman" (not "sailor") has his "wonynge" (residing, cf. German *wohnen*), "far by west," clothes of "falding" (an Irish wool and an Irish-derived word),[18] and almost no words from French except his dagger's "laas" (cord; cf. *lace*, as in *shoelace*).

As the Irish falding nicely suggests, English is not only half-Latinate half-German either. As a mercantile language, stripped of many endings and other grammatical markers as a way of reconciling the initial clash of Norman French and Anglo-Saxon, it has long been famously adept at borrowing and acquiring vocabulary from other world languages. While it isn't a case of translation per se, let me end this chapter by describing a beautiful short story by the Indian writer Vishwapriya L. Iyengar originally written in English, "No Letter from Mother," about translation, English communication, and the cultural translations and discontinuities of

18. Andrew Breeze, "An Irish Etymology for Chaucer's 'Falding' ('Coarse Woollen Cloth')," *Chaucer Review* 35.1 (2000): 112–114.

the main character, a girl at an international boarding school in India in the 1960s.[19] It reinforces the idea that no language is monolingual.

We hear in the story about rajnigandha growing at the Madonna's feet, or someone eating "English toffees from Kenya," or "Zarina from Zambia . . . passing a stick of Wrigley's Spearmint to Bina from Calcutta." The first quoted dialogue in the story is:

> "Holy Mary Mother of Christ, blessed is the fruit of thy
> womb . . ." I was late.
> "Always late," Sister Francis screamed, "in her last janam
> she must have been a tortoise."

This is funny—the Catholic nun screaming about Hindu reincarnation—and it mixes languages in the literal sense too, not just discourses or voices: *janam* is Hindi, not English, or at least not in the *OED*. But English has always done this: other words Iyengar uses, like *dhobi* for a washerwoman, and *dhow*, and *brinjal*, are now "inside" "English" "proper." One girl, who is key to the plot of the story, has a dress with "French chiffon pleated ruffles, but they looked shabby with washing, the dhobi had burned the fabric a bit, so it wasn't 'foreign-foreign.'" This French chiffon dress—something foreign, burned by its contact with another culture, and no longer foreign-foreign—is just like the borrowed Hindi word *dhobi*,

19. In *In Other Words: New Writing by Indian Women* (Kali for Women, 1992).

and the borrowed French word *chiffon*, and the Anglo-Indian grammar of *foreign-foreign*.

Central to the story is that all the girls look forward to letters from their parents, including the narrator. Her father's letters are a somewhat dry anthology, "full of anecdotes from Birbal, Tenali Raman and Kautilya" or "Gladstone or Disraeli"; they sound "a little boring, like Nehru." Still, they're all she has, because "Mother never wrote me letters. Mother was always reading Kannada novels by women late at night." (Kannada is one of the official languages of India, in the same family as Tamil.) As the narrator says near the end: "I was too young to realize that colonisation had cut the bond twixt mother and child." Yet the story rebuilds these broken bonds. Her mother would read these Kannada novels out loud late at night, "when the house had been quilted to sleep in a soft blend of mixed breathing." The narrator remembers one passage and gives it in the story itself, seamlessly incorporated with no indentation, no quotation marks or other signs of citation, and, if we believe the fiction, apparently translated invisibly from Kannada into English. The passage becomes part of the story, with imagery and style that spill over into the story as a whole; translation is integrated into the original text. When the narrator finally does get a letter from Mother, belying the story's title, it has none of her mother's trademark spicy metaphors—"I cannot write in English," the letter bluntly says. "Your teachers will make fun of my English so I will not write again to you"—but by the time the narrator tells the story, she has learned how to speak in her mother's voice, or with it, in a soft blend of mixed breathing.

Iyengar's point, and mine, is that language is not pure and cleanly delimited, even in a monolingual context or in a so-called source language or target language. And with this we are back at the idea that we translate utterances: not words of a language, not anything that can be described as purely linguistic. Naturally, Iyengar's story isn't evidence for anything except that she describes or constructs the English language as hybrid and polylingual. But this lesson is true to my experience as a translator: everything I do is a case of believing that one language can and always will carry traces of another, that the boundaries are permeable, and that (in my case) English is capacious enough for "other" languages. The idea of making English be something non-English is alien to my experience as a translator, and to that of every translator I know of. When I read like a translator, I see what the original author is doing with and to their language; when I write, I am trying to activate and exploit the capacities of English; by yoking the two, I deny the isolated monolinguality of both languages. The original text, like Iyengar's characters' words and Johnson's and Faulkner's and Conrad's languages, is inherently able to enter a newly enriched and expanded English, and English is inherently able to welcome it in.

When it comes to translation, nothing is foreign-foreign.

6

TRANSLATING FORCE

When we translate an utterance for the "arc"—the way that it deviates from the baseline of the unremarkable standard or the cold, dead cliché—what exactly are we trying to capture? How do we preserve what the utterance is doing, how it's moving?

I have come to think of this as a process of translating the *force* of the language. Gertrude Stein said something that I think about a lot: "It is not clarity that is desirable but force," which she also called "vitality." She wrote in her inimitably forceful fashion that "clarity is of no importance because nobody listens and nobody knows what you mean, nor how clearly you mean what you mean," but if you have "vitality enough" to know what you do mean, or at least know enough about what you mean, then people will have no choice but to accept the fact that you do mean something, namely what you're saying, and this "is as near as anybody can come to understanding anyone."[1] What matters is not the clarity of a translation but its force.

In physics, force is energy directionally applied, and I would like to point out here, again, the directionality of a text: not the "arrow" of its address to a literal audience, but the "arc" of its movement from the "baseline." The text is a use of language that exerts force, actualizes various potentials in the language, emphasizes or even invents things that the language can do. The utterance looked at in this way isn't a thought, message, or action being communicated *through* language: it is a piece of language that *does* something, and not just to the reader but also to the language as a whole. In a translation, even what look like divergences or outright mistakes on the single-word level may well be part of what you need to do to re-create the same force in English.

When I retranslated Max Weber's so-called "Vocation Lectures," given as popular lectures in late 1917 and early 1919, I tried to make them sound like popular lectures in English too. Academic German is a laborious, involuted style— admittedly, academic English is not always of the snappiest, but vigorous, direct writing is desirable there as well. The earlier translations of Weber, even the better ones, had literal versions of his German such as "We can see very clearly

1. From her late work *Four in America* (1933; first published by Yale University Press, 1947), p. 127; the passage is more easily available in *Writings and Lectures, 1909–1945*, ed. Patricia Meyerowitz (Penguin, 1967), p. 300.

that the latest developments are moving in the same direction as . . ." (*Nun können wir . . . mit Deutlichkeit beobachten: daß die neueste Entwicklung . . . in der Richtung der [X] verläuft*), which I translated as "The clear trend is toward" (five words instead of sixteen). Or: "Let us begin by making clear what is meant in practice by . . ." (*Machen wir uns zunächst klar, was denn eigentlich [X] praktisch bedeutet*), which became "Let me first clarify" (twelve words now four). How should we describe the difference between these translations?

A standard thing to say, going back to Cicero, Horace, and Saint Jerome, would be that you can translate word for word, which is bad, or translate for the meaning, which is good. In these terms, though, we have no way to say that the shorter Weber translations are good, only a way to say that the longer translations are somewhat word for word, hence bad. Yet it doesn't seem quite relevant to talk about the meaning at all here. These Weber phrases are entirely rhetorical, with no real content: they basically exist solely to move the listeners/readers along and prepare them for the next step in Weber's argument.

Many practicing translators argue that we translate to create the same *effect* in the translation as in the original. The clearest confirmation of this definition is the case of humor: if there's a joke in the original, we have to put humor in the translation, and it doesn't matter if our new joke has different literal content than the original joke. I think this claim is true as far as it goes, but doesn't go far enough. "Effect" is a directional idea, like intentionality: the "same" effect won't be the same effect if it's aimed at a different group of readers. If you say you're translating to create the same effect, that risks sounding like you're working on the text (its words, its meaning, its effect), but really you're working to set up a relationship with the new readers—that's where the "effect" happens.

If anything, the relational aspect is predominant. In our Weber case, it's not entirely clear that the translation *is* creating the same effect as the original—it's that the effect of the German prose works well on German listeners but badly on English readers. The only way to argue that "Let me first clarify" has the same effect as "Let us begin by making clear what is meant in practice by" is to zoom out quite far and say that the effect is "it sounds good to its listeners" (English listeners in the former case, German listeners in the latter). Which makes the concept of "translating for the effect" rather useless. The German sounds right to the German audience, and we want the English to sound right to the English audience, and that rightness depends on the listener's or reader's expectations (of the genre of published lecture) more than on the text's intrinsic effects. What we're doing is aiming the Weber at the new audience in a way that reflects how it was directed at the original audience.

This is a simple example precisely because it's rhetorical: the translation obviously needs to pay attention to the relationship with, or address to, the reader, since all this sentence is doing is managing that relationship. Things get more complicated when we're translating a passage with more substance, or even literary quality. Here is the first sentence of

"The Freeloader," the first story in my translation of Nescio's *Amsterdam Stories*. Nescio is the writer who swept away stuffy literary formality and brought idiomatic, spoken verve into Dutch writing over a century ago, comparable to Mark Twain in American English, and this is one of the most famous sentences in Dutch literature, in a story practically every Dutch person has read, about a nationally beloved character. Think "Call me Ishmael" spoken by Holden Caulfield in *The Great Gatsby*. No pressure.

> *Behalve den man, die de Sarphatistraat de mooiste plek van Europa vond, heb ik nooit een wonderlijker kerel gekend dan den uitvreter.*

> Except for the man who thought Sarphatistraat was the most beautiful place in Europe, I've never met anyone more peculiar than the freeloader.

(Nescio has a sentimental attachment to the neighborhood around Sarphatistraat, in the east part of Amsterdam, but it is not by any objective measure a sightseeing destination; this unnamed man more peculiar than the freeloader is never mentioned again. Some of Nescio's original readers will have recognized the contemporary cultural figure he is glancingly alluding to; most of his later readers will not.)

Nearly every word here except the "the"s raises a translation issue. The dictionary definitions are all clear enough and the words all have one-word equivalents in English, but the translator has to capture what Virginia Woolf called "the whole fling of the sentence"—another synonym, perhaps, for Stein's "force." Others might call this the text's *voice*, typically thought of as a matter of tone, register, rhythm, and other musical analogies, but I would say it's an interpersonal, directional problem: the sentence introduces three people—the Sarphatistraat fan, the freeloader, and the speaker—and addresses itself to a fourth, and what's most important in the sentence are the relations it sets up among these people. Is Nescio, or the narrator, making fun of the Sarphatistraat fan, or secretly agreeing, and if so, agreeing defiantly or insinuating that deep down you know you agree too? (He assumes that you are familiar enough with this figure in some sense that he can bring him up and never mention him again.) And then how does the qualification about that man set up or prejudice your expectations about the way the freeloader is remarkable—marvelous or just bizarre? Wondrous or crazy?

A more literal translation of the sentence is: "Leaving aside the man who found Sarphatistraat the most beautiful spot in Europe, I have never known a stranger fellow than the freeloader." As we saw in many examples last chapter, synonymous options abound: is it the *prettiest, loveliest, most beautiful*, or *nicest spot in, corner of, nook in all of*, or *place in* Europe? *Mooi*, like the German word *schön*, means "beautiful" in the most elevated, sublime sense but is also, as a nice one-syllable word, used more blandly to mean "pretty," "cool," "neat," all the way down to nearly meaningless interjections like "uh-huh" or "okay." The word is extremely common, and every time it comes up the translator has to decide not what it means but where to pitch it. A *plek*, cognate with English "fleck," is a spot or patch, as on clothing, and also a small area, zone, geographical spot. Has the narrator never met an odder *fellow* or *chap* (the dictionary definitions of *kerel*), *guy* (more idiomatic but arguably too contemporary), *man*, or *person*, or do we dodge the word altogether and say "anyone" (or "anybody")? Even the first word of the sentence, a striking and slightly fussy opener since it starts by pushing away, by excepting or excluding someone we've never heard of anyway, confronts the translator with choices: *Leaving aside, Disregarding, Save for*, or the simpler *Aside from, Except for, Other than*? The "freeloader" himself—the title of the story—is the *uitvreter*, literally "out-gobbler," someone who snatches up everything you've got, eats you out of house and home. The closest translation I can think of is *schnorrer*, but the Yiddishism is too jarring; other possible translations include *sponger* and *leech* (both metaphors of sucking dry and thus closer to the original), and *mooch*, but all of these sound old fashioned in kind of the wrong way. Lesser dilemmas are involved with every verb in the sentence. The man "found" Sarphatistraat the most beautiful place in Europe: is it important to keep the metaphor of searching, or is this construction too formal in English? The narrator has never "known" an odder fellow, implying longer acquaintance, not just running into him, but "met" is more natural in English. If you want to count the auxiliary "have" as a verb, there's an issue there too: contraction or no contraction? Nescio is famous in Dutch for his original use of contractions, though not in this sentence; the particular verb form here (*heb ik*) isn't subject to contraction in Dutch, so Nescio didn't choose to avoid the contraction and *I have* and *I've* are equally correct translations.

There are dozens, hundreds of permutations, and each one will resonate differently with everything else in the rest of the page, the story, the book. So you place your bet and you take your chances. Dutch speakers will tell you—believe me, they'll tell you—that *spot* is the "correct" translation for *plek*; there is another Dutch word, *plaats*, for "place." So why use "place"? The choice can't be defended on the level of the individual word. "Spot" isn't wrong for *plek* and doesn't "sound wrong" in a usual sense, and actually it's better in some ways, since it's more chatty, like *plek*. But it throws the sentence out of tune somehow: maybe because *Sarphatistraat* is more alien and unfamiliar to an English reader than a Dutch reader, so for balance we need the least obtrusive word for *plek*; maybe because "spot" is too casual to go with the elevated "most beautiful" (whereas "prettiest spot" or the like wouldn't make the man seem quite as unique, especially to readers who don't know anything about Sarphatistraat); maybe because "Except for" is a straightforward translation of *Behalve*, so the sentence needs less colloquializing down; maybe because the contraction "I've" does the colloquializing work already (partly to set up the polysyllabic "peculiar"). I don't completely believe any of these explanations.

The analogy to music has crept in again: "resonate," "out of tune." That's not quite what I mean. The sentence with "spot" grabs you less; it casts this peculiar fellow as peculiar in a hair's-breadth different way and thus sets up your feelings for the freeloader differently, speaks to you differently as a whole. It has a different force. It comes up to you, comes on to you, grabs you by the collar and gets in your face differently—there is a good French word for this, *aborder*: to board a ship, to grapple, to make landfall or reach a port, to tackle a question, and also to come up to, accost, or hit on a person. I'm not sure whether to call this "arrow" or "arc," and it probably doesn't matter: the opening line in translation is now addressing English speakers, but intrinsic to the literary nature of the text, its "arc" from the baseline of language, is its interpersonal address, its approach, its come-on to the reader.

Along with the orientation toward an audience, and of course the literal meaning, what, then, are we translating for? I would distinguish four qualities: sound, register, association, and movement.

(I) SOUND. The most famous slogan in Weber's "Vocation Lecture" on politics, especially inspiring to those who toil away doing the hard, unflashy work of making political change happen, is "*Die Politik bedeutet ein starkes langsames Bohren von harten Brettern mit Leidenschaft und Augenmaß zugleich,*" especially the first ten words. "Politics means a hard, slow boring into hard boards." Unfortunately, the repetition of "hard" (meaning "forceful," then meaning "solid"), which doesn't exist in the German (*starkes, harten*), as well as the requirement of elegant variation, demands that we use a synonym for one or the other. "Politics means a slow, laborious boring into hard boards": here the English words "la*bor*ious" and "*bor*ing" and "*bor*ds," though completely unrelated etymologically, make the phrase sound ridiculous. My eventual translation, "Politics is a slow and difficult drilling of holes into hard boards," is less than ideal in several ways: "drilling" gives less of a suggestion of hard muscular labor than "boring" does (I, at least, have a picture flash into my mind of an effortless electric drill); "laborious" emphasizes the struggle of the work, while "difficult" raises issues of eventual success or failure; it's less snappy to say "drilling of holes into" instead of "boring into." But these concessions have to be made because of the quirks of how the syllables of the English words sound.

The need to avoid adding extraneous sound qualities in prose is just the inverse of the obvious demands of translating rhyming poetry, song, and wordplay. When Stephen Sondheim in *Into the Woods* has Jack's mother tell Jack to take their old cow to market as soon as possible, for "we've no time to sit and dither / while her withers wither with her," any decent translation needs to sound like bored board-boring even if the word in the other language for the ridge between a quadruped's shoulder blades has no homophones. When translating one of the Swiss writer Robert Walser's jingly couplets, for instance this one:

Nun sitzt die Zage genau wie solch ein Mann da,
nichtsdestoweniger grüße ich dich herzlich, kleine liebe Wanda

the sound outranks the meaning and we are willing to lose the name of the addressee, "dear little Wanda," and even the fact that she is who the speaker is writing to, in order to keep the silly rhyme:

> And now the shy lady sits there like such a man does,
> nonetheless I send you my warmest greetings, along with Amanda's.

(II) REGISTER. It is especially obvious in dialogue that the words a character speaks have to sound as if that character might speak them—children need to sound like children, no matter how precocious; fluent English speakers don't speak in clunky translationese. But the text as a whole, with its implied author, is pitched at a certain level, and the translation likewise has to be not too technical and arcane, not too chatty or dumbed down.

In Victoria Kielland's novel *My Men*, the rich, callow young man on the nineteenth-century Norwegian farm who takes advantage of a servant girl is referred to as Odelen. This is not a normal name in Norwegian, but the word is capitalized here to function as a name; *odelen* means "the property owned under an allodial system." I didn't know what that meant either; it turns out that an allodial system is one in which "land is held 'in allodium' rather than by any superior landlord," or in other words it's the opposite of feudalism, under which system an overlord or sovereign holds tenurial rights. There are two English words for this type of property, *allod* (used mostly in a medieval context) and *allodium*, but

I had never run across either word in my life, while *odelen* in Norwegian, according to my research (and asking the author), is less obscure, comparable in tone to "feudalism" in English: it's specific, but people generally know more or less what it means. Naming the character Allod would completely obscure Kielland's wonderful literary gesture, which so emphasizes the young man's social position and impersonal power. I thus looked for a different term in English, one suggestive of unearned privilege, not a name, and legalistic but still comprehensible. I ended up with phrases and sentences like "She looked at Firstborn and felt a single long breath move through her body," "Firstborn with his big blond curls and squeaking boots," "Firstborn came back, a huge mass of skin and a wide white smile, so addicted to his own desire." Primogeniture is not the same as an allodial system, but the translation didn't have to mean the same thing—it had to be in the same register in order to do the same work, hit readers the same way.

When English (or whatever the translating language is) doesn't have the same registers as the original language, that poses another problem. Some languages—I know of Austro-Hungarian German and Japanese—have many more linguistic ways of expressing politeness, respect, or obedience than English does, and a more or less formulaic phrase in the original ("most honored and esteemed sir"), if translated literally, would sound fawning, ridiculous, or at best eighteenth century ("Your obedient servant"). We have to express politeness in our own language, even if the language is less polite.

So too, every translator from a less puritan language into
English has struggled with the fact that the English words for
sex and sexual anatomy sound either clinical and technical or
vulgar and insulting, sometimes to the point of taboo (fella-
tio or blow job, penis or cock, vagina or the c-word), while
the original language is often able to describe such things in a
more casual and acceptable register.

Relatedly, there is the language of intentional insult and
obscenity, which is entirely a matter of register. Like Weber's
rhetorical gestures, curse words like "asshole" or "mother-
fucker" function solely by addressing the reader or listener in a
certain way—when used as insults, they do not literally denote
a body part or activity. And the decision of how to translate
an insult depends on how it will strike readers or listeners in
the translating language. In a review of an English translation
of five early modern Bengali tales, the eminent scholar Wendy
Doniger at first admits that it "jarred upon my ears" to encounter fully vernacular translations, "accustomed as I am to both
writing and reading translations that (especially when published in India) avoid obscenity," even by omitting the words
if need be. Six times in the book under review, a character
calls someone a "daughter-fucker" or "sister-fucker," literal
translations according to Doniger of the Bengla *beti-cod* and
shala. She recognizes, though, that choosing "the best register in which to translate these terms" depends on not just the
original genre and the fictional speaker's status "but also the
social class and moment in history of the reader." In the end,

she praises the translator for his "brave and vivid choice" of how to position the text in English.[2]

(III) ASSOCIATION. In Jon Fosse's *Septology*, the main character picks up and reads a small-town newspaper published elsewhere, not in the big city where he's reading it; that paper is called in Norwegian *Gula Tidend*, literally *Gula Times*. This name said nothing to me, and Googling Gula turned up Gulen, an obscure town in Norway. So I asked Fosse about it, and he emailed me back: "*Gula* is an old verb meaning a wind blowing strongly, and it was also the name for a region in Norway during the Middle Ages, the Viking Era; the most famous old Norwegian law is from this region, '*gulatingslova.*' Gula is also the name of an island in this region." He did not tell me that he had worked as a journalist for the real *Gula Tidend* while in college, something I found out only later— he must have felt that the biographical fact wasn't important. He suggested that I use whatever sounded best in English in the context of the novel: "It could also be something like the Country (?) Times or something like that." This suggestion was helpful because it encouraged me not to worry about the literal meaning and prompted me to think solely about the associations he'd mentioned—strong wind, medieval law, outlying rural place—and what words, clearly recognizable as

2. Wendy Doniger, "Of Crocodiles and Kings," *New York Review of Books*, May 11, 2023, p. 57, reviewing *Needle at the Bottom of the Sea: Bengali Tales from the Land of the Eighteen Tides*, tr. Tony K. Stewart (University of California Press, 2023).

a newspaper name, would most bring them to mind. In the fictional context of the novel, I ended up calling the paper *The Northern Herald*, semisubliminally evoking medieval heralds and heraldry and the distant Viking north. This was a case where no other demand outweighed the value of keeping the associations for English readers as comparable as possible to the Norwegian readers'.

We have to pay attention not only to the original's associations but also to the translation's. Fosse's latest novella, about an everyman figure wandering in a forest, getting lost, and encountering presences who appear as shining auras of pure white, is called *Kvitleik*, which means "whiteness": *kvit* = white; *-leik* is the ending that turns an adjective into a noun. However, calling an English-language book *Whiteness* in the 2020s would suggest a whole universe of concerns around racial privilege. A race-sensitive reading of Fosse's *Kvitleik* is of course possible and interesting, but it would be very misleading to suggest to readers that race is what the book is primarily about. Since "Whiteness" has other associations in the English-speaking world today, it can't be the title here; the publishers and I went with *A Shining*, taking advantage of still other associations not in the Norwegian, but this time suitable (spooky Stephen King and Stanley Kubrick).

The word "association" nicely means both the ideas a word evokes and the relations a word maintains with other words it has dealings with. A word's circle of friends and cabal of enemies—we really can't say "circle of enemies" and "cabal of friends," and that's the point. Beyond all discernable logic or arguments about the real world (why *not* have a circle of enemies?), there are simply things you can say in one language that are not said the same way in another. Jacques Barzun describes the phenomenon well in his witty, exasperated book *An Essay on French Verse: For Readers of English Poetry*, where he tries to show a prejudiced public, inclined to say that there was no good French poetry before modernism, how to read French properly. At one point he remarks:

> In all images and epithets we see the wilfulness of language once
> more at work. . . . English critics of French literature have often
> exclaimed at the silliness even of epithets in common locutions.
> One I happen to remember made merry over a novelist's *une
> après-midi adorable*—who can adore an afternoon? He might
> have been answered: "Tell us how the weather can be *glorious*?"
> which to a French ear verges on the idiotic.

I admit that it is hard for me to feel even a hint of any problem with "glorious weather," but I believe Barzun, imagining he feels about this just what I feel about "a lovable afternoon."

A translation thus often has to recast the phrase. Giving the example of the first line of a sonnet by Mallarmé, *"La chair est triste, hélas! et j'ai lu tous les livres,"* Barzun elaborates:

> The "sadness of the flesh" gets by, but "I have read all the
> books" totally lacks the evocative power of the original; as
> an image it is inert. An approximation would be: "and all
> knowledge is stale." The reason why the literal sense fails

to convey this feeling lies in the aura of *livres*; the word is weightier, more charged with reverence than *books*. In "I've read all the books," one hears a schoolboy, not a philosopher.[3]

That is, the associations of "knowledge" come closer to the associations of *livre*.

One subcategory of association perhaps worth emphasizing is the issue of anachronism. A translation is always of an utterance not only in a different language but from an earlier time, whether centuries or a few seconds ago. Words sometimes have strong associations with a specific era, the way "groovy" evokes the 1960s. Sometimes words are objectively associated with a specific era whether or not they read that way to general readers, and if used in a book about a different era they will stick out to the better-informed reader. For instance, "gravitational center" was not used until the 1950s; "center of gravity" was used instead, going back to the nineteenth century. Saying "gravitational center" in a historical novel set in the nineteenth century will be jarring to certain readers.[4]

3. Both passages are from *An Essay on French Verse: For Readers of English Poetry* (New Directions, 1991), p. 72. Daniel Hahn similarly but more extensively discusses the different associations of *book* (rhymes with *crook* and *nook*; visually rhymes with *boo* and *moon* and *food*; also means make a reservation) and *livre* (like freedom in the form of *libre*; weight and heavy money, *livre*; lips, *lèvres*; rhymes with drunk, *ivre*) in *Catching "Fire": A Translation Diary* (Charco, 2022), pp. 6–7.

4. Such as the writer Brandon Taylor, who complained on Twitter about this usage of "gravitational center." I hadn't known that the term was anachronistic, but luckily had never used it.

Some translators like to use resources such as the *OED* to make sure that when translating a foreign work from, say, 1910, they use only words that were in English usage in 1910. Personally, I find this strategy a bit incoherent. I have never seen a modern translator put *Don Quixote* into Elizabethan English, and what about translating Homer or Ovid, written before the English language existed? There seems to be an invisible cutoff, in the eighteenth century or thereabouts, before which everyone knows that there's no point in trying to match the age of the words—at most, you can use the Ezra Pound "Seafarer" strategy and make the language sound more or less like ye olde literary Englisshe. This lack of universal applicability points up that the strategy as a whole is kind of a gimmick. Some words are associated with a certain time and some aren't; using words that existed in 1910 won't by itself make your text feel like 1910, and using words that didn't exist then won't necessarily ruin the effect either (assuming that that's the effect you're going for—usually translators do want to avoid anachronism, but sometimes they want to emphasize the present-day relevance of an older text, especially one without time-bound local color, like a philosophy treatise or an animal fable). Most problematic of all is the overarching fact that these Spanish or Chinese or Greek authors and characters weren't speaking English originally, and yet they are speaking English in the translation! English from 1910 is a language no closer to the foreign original than present-day English is.

It is also true that a translator isn't necessarily trying to make the associations of the translation match the original's as closely as possible. A best-selling Korean memoir of depression and therapy by Baek Sehee is called in Anton Hur's translation *I Want to Die but I Want to Eat Tteokbokki*; the cover shows a depressed-looking young Asian woman facedown on her low bed, reaching down with a pair of chopsticks toward a dish of food on the floor. *Tteokbokki* is a word that will mean nothing to many English-language readers, and to those readers its associations are, roughly speaking, "exotic" plus "they don't care if I understand the title," rather than "yummy comfort food." On the other hand, adding the verb—not calling the book *I Want to Die but I Want Tteokbokki*—tells English-language readers that tteokbokki is a kind of food (as does the cover). Since the book was recommended by BTS, one of the biggest bands in the world, and that is a prominent part of its marketing in English, Hur can assume that Baek's readers in English have a decent chance of knowing what tteokbokki is via their love of K-pop, whether or not they're K-pop fans due to a preexisting familiarity with Korean culture. But for readers who don't know the word, Hur's choice, like much of his translation work, is an intervention designed to expand what they know and how they expect to be addressed, not to accept and work within those constraints. If Hur's goal were to slavishly match the literal meaning of the original, he might have called the book *I Want to Die but I Want to Eat Korean Spicy Rice Cakes*; if his goal were to slavishly match the associations of the original, he might have called it . . . *but I Also Want Donuts* or . . . *a Big Plate of Spaghetti*. Needless to say, these are terrible translations. The point is that Hur knows he is writing for a different audience than the original's—more exactly, for a heterogeneous audience that only partly overlaps the original Korean book's heterogeneous audience. The book is different for this audience, it is being marketed differently and it will be read differently, and different associations are necessary and appropriate.

(IV) MOVEMENT. Languages exist at particular moments of historical time, but any given piece of language is also inherently temporal: the words come in a certain order.

Here is my favorite sentence by Robert Walser:

> *Der weite See glich einem Kinde, das völlig still ist, weil es schläft und träumt.*

> The large lake resembled a child who is completely silent because asleep and dreaming.

The beauty of this idea is how it's ordered.[5] How can a large lake be like a child—isn't smallness what defines a child? It

---

5. The translator and writer Jennifer Croft's essay on the "microsuspense" in every sentence that makes us want to keep reading similarly reminds us that every piece of language is a choreographed movement in time: "The reader has to live the process of apprehension, experience a world in an order, not all at once"; "part of an idea is how it's ordered" ("The Order of Things: Jennifer Croft on Translating Olga Tokarczuk," Literary Hub, February 1, 2022, https://www .lithub.com/the-order-of-things-jennifer-croft-on-translating-olga-tokarczuk/, also appearing as "Micro-suspense and the Desire to Keep Reading: Translating Olga Tokarczuk's *The Books of Jacob*," in *The Routledge World Companion to Polish Literature*, ed. Tomasz Bilczewski, Stanley Bill, and Magdalena Popiel [Routledge, 2021], pp. 428–438).

turns out they are alike in their silence, even though neither
form of life is generally known for being completely silent. The
child is silent because asleep, which explains that part. But
the child is dreaming . . . and with that a universe opens back
up, within the child who is large after all, containing worlds
wider than even the largest lake. The animate child is stilled
and then brought back to life, an inaccessible inner life. I am
happy for this child; I love this child, as much as Walser loves
and makes me love his lake.

The sentence comes in the middle of a series of such reversals, all helping to set us afloat in Walser's dreamworld:

> The high mountain, drawn down by gentle forces, sank mildly
> with a wonderful gesture into the depths, where the smooth
> surface of the water gracefully reflected it. The large lake
> resembled a child who is completely silent because asleep
> and dreaming. The calm reigning everywhere all around was
> made yet stronger, and bigger, by the delicate rush of the rain;
> the silence, rustling noiselessly back and forth like an evening
> bird, experienced no lessening from the timorous light wind
> shyly wafting from the west.

Sinking and rising, back and forth, big strong calmness, rus-
tling silence. It may not matter what the opposites are—maybe
the pattern itself is enough. I never get tired of replaying these
reversals in my mind. They open something up inside me, an
inner sky, as Rilke calls it. The alternation sets up two opposing poles, pulls them as far apart as possible, and maintains

the tension or communication between them—in the back-and-forth, the space between, is where the feeling lives. This dreamy dizziness feels like what art is.

Insofar as it's possible to distinguish the two, I am talking here about the movement of the description, not the movement of the language: the content, not rhythm or scanning. But of course rhythm matters too, in prose as well as poetry. Walser's German sentence has a harmonious balance, with the three comma-separated parts, each alternating stressed and unstressed syllables, each ending on an unstressed syllable and a pause, until the strong finish. An optional, slightly archaic word form—*Kinde* instead of *Kind*—makes the pattern perfect. Here's how the syllables scan:

× / × / × / × / ×
Der weite See glich einem Kinde,

× / × / ×
das völlig still ist,

× × / × /
weil es schläft und träumt.

I don't scan sentences as I translate; I had never scanned this one until the translation was done and I realized how much the sentence moved me. If I'd done it beforehand, I could have matched the syllables in English—

The spacious lake was like a child who
is wholly silent
while he sleeps and dreams

—but that wouldn't have been a better sentence in this case, especially since it forces a gender onto our sleeping mystery. My intuitive translation matched Walser's two-beat phrases and had a rhythm of its own, ending in a doubled pattern of rushed rise and quick falling off:

> × /   /
> The large lake

> × /   × ×   /
> resembled a child

> × ×   ×   /   × /×
> who is completely silent

> × ×   × / ×   /   ×
> because asleep and dreaming.

If we had a grammar of prose rhythm, we would know more about the difference between Walser's dreams in German and in translation, or maybe children's dreams in German and in English. The German is stately and regular, a march with a pause for each change in direction; the English starts stronger and fades gently and evenly away, like the splash and ripples of a stone tossed into a large lake. In any case, the translation needs an order, a movement, somehow comparable to the original's.[6]

---

6. I like these explanations of rhythm (a stately march, stronger, like a splash), although underneath it all I am somewhat skeptical: they feel a bit like projection, or reverse-engineering an explanation from a feeling. If I wanted to, couldn't I equally well call regular two-beat phrases "soothing and lulling"? Like Bakhtin, who denied the existence of a word's "color" or intrinsic "music," Barzun makes

* * *

Sound, register, association, and movement. They all came up even in the case of translating proper names: Brage should be Bragi for the sound; Odelen should be Firstborn, not Allod, for the register; Sitting Bull, Little Snow, or She-Who-Builds-with-Wood have the wrong amount of association; movement generally takes place across larger stretches of language, but you could say that the accents in Ugrešić and Tȟatȟáŋka create roadblocks that slow the English-language reader down, whereas a lack of accents promotes swifter movement.

Does it help to label and list these four qualities? They are not entirely distinct: I sometimes feel that "sound" is the most general category and everything else falls under "what the text sounds like." Issues of scanning, sentence rhythm, and word order could certainly go there as well as under "movement." The acoustics of the text is so much of what matters in a translation and so little of what people usually talk about: translations are always reviewed and praised or criticized in terms of their accuracy, or perhaps faithfulness, when the sound of the thing is what makes or breaks it, the same as with anything else one reads. Sometimes I think of "association" as the umbrella term—how a word associates with other words

---

this point: "Onomatopoeia is a fiction." He says that the actual meaning produces what we pretend comes from the sound—Pope's "Soft is the strain" definitely sounds gentle, but the nearly identical sounds in "Tough is the strain" convey harsh groaning; "celandine," a flower, sounds much lovelier than a prosaic but sonically very similar "cellardoor" (*Essay on French Verse*, p. 51).

determines the movement through the sentence;[7] sound and register too are part of "what the text makes the reader think of." Maybe separating these four qualities could help create a kind of checklist, but the working translator would rarely if ever run down the list—they will attend to all these aspects of their writing at once. My experience at least, of reading like a translator and translating, is one of opening up my attention to as much as I possibly can, both of what I'm reading and of my own responses to it, and anticipating as much as I can how the English-language reader might react to anything and everything in what I produce.

It's a bit of a stretch, but we could also map these four qualities onto the four components of the French word *sens* and Merleau-Ponty's account of intentionality: sound = the sensory aspect; register = how commonsensical or sensible it is; association = the meaning or sense; movement = the direction. An earlier version of this chapter was organized around the idea of "translating for the *sens*," although I ended up deciding that pinning the nature of translation to four meanings of a French word was overly clever rather than helpful. My fifth term, the quintessence of translation, really contains them all: the vitality of the writing moving in a certain direction, its FORCE.

---

7. Croft's essay on microsuspense and sentence movement ("The Order of Things") also discusses association: "A word's intersubjective facet is how it behaves in a phrase and how it interacts with its neighbors. . . . Very few words function well on their own."

Thomas Mann's great story "Unordnung und frühes Leid" was translated into English by H. T. Lowe-Porter in the 1920s as "Disorder and Early Sorrow." I feel that this title is too wan and genteel. *Order* is a more sweeping, cosmic concept in German than it generally is in English, and the absence of order, *Unordnung*, is correspondingly huge—"disorder" sounds like a vase is an inch out of place, or a shelf needs dusting, while *Unordnung* means the time is out of joint, everything topsy-turvy, society plunged into madness. In Mann's title, referring to the German hyperinflation and social turmoil of the early 1920s, it is somewhat arch but not minimizing.[8] I settled for a while on "Disarray and Early Suffering," which more actively suggests a prior state of organization being disrupted and ruined; it gets closer in connotation to the German while recognizably corresponding to Lowe-Porter's earlier title, but it doesn't sound very good. In the end, since English wants adjectives or verbs with active subjects instead of German's abstract nouns, I changed *Unordnung* into an adjective and supplied a less conceptual noun, omitting the expected article to keep a little of Mann's generality, and ended up with "Chaotic World and Childhood Sorrow." The words are now more forceful: a chaotic world is more chaotic than "chaos," childhood sorrow is sadder than "early sorrow"—not logically, but in English.

---

8. The other words in the title pose other problems; see my introduction to Thomas Mann, *New Selected Stories*, tr. Damion Searls (Liveright, 2023), for further discussion.

One final example, again from Uwe Johnson's *Anniversaries*. Describing the waves on the Baltic, a memory recalled to the German character's mind by the waves at the New Jersey shore, the novel's opening paragraph in the original ends: "*Das Wort für die kurzen Wellen der Ostsee ist kabbelig gewesen.*" I couldn't find "*kabbelig*" in any dictionary. The earlier, partial translation of the novel had said: "The word for the short waves of the Baltic was *choppity*." And I thought, That's pretty good, it's a new word to me but I know what it means, it's like *choppy*. That's the word I put in my draft, and then I moved on. In fact, the printed galleys of *Anniversaries* say "choppity." But at some point, near the end of the translation process, after the galleys were printed, I thought: Wait, that's wrong. It's not *choppity*. And I don't know what the criteria were for making this decision, because *kabbelig* is nothing but a word that has the definition Johnson says it has: the translation could be anything ("The word we used for the waves was 'blibberblub'"). But a translator has to make unjustifiable decisions too. "Choppity" just suddenly seemed to me too Beatrix Potter, it made me think "hippity hoppity bippity boppity." It also seemed too English as opposed to American. It was *not* the energy of this Baltic memory bursting into the character's experience as she's swimming in New Jersey. So instead I went with "The word for the short waves on the Baltic was: *scrabbly*."

This too is not a word I had ever heard applied to waves, but you get what it means, and it has a different energy, or vitality, about it. It's a different kind of experience. I later went to the *OED* and German etymological dictionaries to see if I could reverse-engineer a good reason for having picked this word, and sure enough I could. *Kabbelig* is of course very similar sonically to *scrabbly*, and such similarity doesn't always mean anything, but German and English are pretty close, so it sometimes means something. There's also *Kabbelei*, and a verb form *kabbeln*, which means "to squabble, quarrel, have a scrappy little argument," and the *scrabbly/scrappy* resonance works well. *Scrabble* in English has various meanings, besides the word game: scribbling, like writing, scribble-scrabble; also scratching around or making raking motions with your hands, which was my main association with the word. Scrambling along, struggling or scrambling for something. Maybe the word game Scrabble is a nice little subliminal gesture toward translation, the task of assembling new words. And *scrabble* isn't an Americanism, but *hardscrabble* is, so it does in a way have a more belligerent and confrontational energy about it.

When I made that change from *choppity* to *scrabbly*, I secretly believe that it changed the whole book. All 1,700 pages were different. I don't literally believe this, but I have to confess that secretly, mystically, I *do* believe it: the whole book is different because it's not choppity, it's scrabbly. My manifesto as a translator, instead of saying Make It New, like Ezra Pound, would be: Make It Scrabbly! Because it's not *clarity* that's desirable, but *force*.

7

TRANSLATING FAITHFULLY

The translation judgments described in the previous chapters must seem somewhat subjective, though I hope the reasons I give for my decisions are convincing. The judgments *are* subjective if by that we mean they are not objective, but my whole account of phenomenology is meant to argue that the terms "subjective" and "objective" don't really apply. (We subjectively see a chair or a sunset, but it is nonetheless objectively a chair or a sunset before our eyes; phrased more rigorously: when we see a chair or sunset, it doesn't make sense to say we are seeing it either subjectively or objectively—what we are doing is seeing it. This is what "seeing it" means.) In translation, the question of objectivity—whether a translation is objectively correct—is the question of whether the translation is faithful. Here too, my argument is that no translation is *either* free *or* faithful. And to make this argument, we have to return to the figure of the translator—the living, breathing, embodied person making their way through a world that also contains the text they translate. We can't treat a translation as dropped from the sky and ask whether or not it's faithful to an impersonal, pre-existing original, any more than we can compare our view of the things of the world to an imagined God's-eye view of them.

Let me begin by considering in some detail a historical example of a debate about faithful translation. M. D. Herter Norton translated nine books by Rainer Maria Rilke, and her version of Rilke's *Letters to a Young Poet* (1934), the first in English, continued as the standard for at least half a century, yet her reputation as a translator has long been rather low, in large part because of how she described herself: she took up the cudgels for faithfully following the original and providing the "closest idiomatic parallel" for it, which often put her in a straw-man position compared to other translators. Once she drew the distinction, in her 1938 foreword to *Translations from the Poetry of Rainer Maria Rilke*, between on the one hand a poem's "*intrinsic* qualities" of content and image and on the other hand the "*technical* elements of form" (i.e., rhyme and meter) and stated her goal of prioritizing the former, she all but invited accusations of being blind to the fact that the language matters.[1]

---

1. These pages are drawn from my foreword to Rilke, *Letters to a Young Poet*, tr. M. D. Herter Norton, Centenary Edition (Norton, 2023), pp. vii–xxv, where I discuss her work in more detail.

A 1975 paper at the Rilke Centennial conference by Ingo
Seidler, published in 1980 and purporting to give an over-
view of Rilke translations into English, shortly before Stephen Mitchell's 1982 *Selected Poetry of Rainer Maria Rilke*
reshaped the landscape of Rilke translations, is partial and
slanted but typical for the time.[2] Seidler defines a continuum
of translators' approaches, with "Mrs Herter Norton's faithful transliterations" (ouch) on one end and "Robert Lowell's
dashing 'imitations'" (dashing!) on the other. Lowell then gets
two and a half pages and several close readings, while Herter
Norton's work is dismissed in half a paragraph:

> This language altogether lacks the sensuous appeal of Rilke's;
> neither his technical brilliance nor his richness, neither his
> music nor his magic, are here preserved. No-one would
> therefore wish to call these renditions poems. . . . To call these
> translations "literary trots" or "prose cribs" would be a trifle
> ungenerous; they are too carefully worked and too sensitively
> balanced. Even so, living poems they are not.

Just a *trifle* ungenerous!

But as is so often the case when someone is alleged to take
an utterly unreasonable position, that position was actually
adopted in the context of a different debate. The Hogarth
Press, run by Virginia and Leonard Woolf, had published

2. "The Reluctant Guest: A Critical Appraisal of English Versions of Rilke,"
Canadian Review of Comparative Literature 7.2 (Spring 1980): 163–173.

Rilke's *Duineser Elegien: Elegies from the Castle at Duino* in 1931, translated by the Woolfs' friends the Sackville-Wests. It was lambasted, then and for the next ninety years, and the widespread criticism by Rilke scholars led Leonard Woolf to choose an academic to translate future Rilke volumes.[3] This was J. B. Leishman, whose many translations won favor at the time for systematically preserving all of Rilke's meters and rhymes, even alternating masculine and feminine rhyme schemes—at the cost, needless to say, of countless extraneous or omitted words and phrases, empty and also likewise purposeless filler, word orders unidiomatic, and oft ludicrous compounds and neologistic thesaurus-ransacking. In one case Leishman uses "deciduous," in a rhyme with "thus," to translate the normal and monosyllabic German word for "tree."

The Sackville-Wests' reviled *Duino Elegies* has recently found its own champions: it was reissued in 2021 with an introduction pointing to its "evident quality." The Sackville-Wests put the *Elegies* entirely into blank verse, resulting in some (though far less) Leishmaniacal padding or trimming without the excuse of copying features of the original. As the new edition points out, though, blank verse is "the most traditional and versatile" English meter, and the Sackville-Wests were thus able to make their English "immediately intelligible and gripping."[4] Today when I read this translation, it doesn't

---

3. See Paulina Choh's essay on Rilke in the Modernist Archives Publishing Project, https://www.modernistarchives.com/person/rainer-maria-rilke.

4. Lesley Chamberlain, introduction to Rilke, *Duino Elegies*, tr. Vita Sackville-West and Edward Sackville-West (1931; Pushkin, 2021), p. 9.

sound like the Rilke I know, but it does sound like good solid traditional poetry, versing blankly on in iambs pure:

> For beauty's nothing but the birth of terror,
> Which we endure but barely, and, enduring,
> Must wonder at it, in that it disdains
> To compass our destruction. Every angel
> Is terrible, and thus in self-control
> I crush the appeal that rises with my sobs.

There is certainly a strong case to be made that their version sounds more like poetry than Leishman's efforts. Poetry from fifty years before its publication date, perhaps, but English poetry nonetheless.

These dueling visions of Rilke don't really fit on Seidler's "continuum" from the faithful Herter Norton to the unfaithful but dashing Lowell. Seidler neglects the Sackville-Wests altogether, calling Leishman and Stephen Spender's 1939 *Duino Elegies* the oldest version in English while unhelpfully putting Leishman "somewhere in between" Herter Norton and Lowell, even though Leishman's slavishness to Rilke's rhyme and meter arguably makes him far more devoted to faithfulness over beauty than Herter Norton. The relevant continuum in the 1930s was really from literary amateurs to academic professionals. Leonard Woolf caved to the predominantly academic English critics and cast his lot with the professionals; Herter Norton took the other side. As a cohead of W. W. Norton publishers, she turned down Leishman's versions of Rilke's *Poems* and *Requiem* and refused to publish his *Duino Elegies* unless Spender was involved. Spender was a successful poet, and he and Leishman quarreled over what to be faithful to, with Spender preferring exact meaning and imagery in loose or irregular meter while Leishman argued that it was more important to keep the rhyme and meter than match the content. In the end they came together and Hogarth published their *Duino Elegies* in 1939, which Norton published in the United States. In this context, Herter Norton arguing for the "closest idiomatic parallel" for a poem's "intrinsic qualities" of content and image was of a piece with insisting that Spender cotranslate the *Duino Elegies*, against Leishman's credentials. It certainly wasn't advocating for "literary trots" or "prose cribs," much less "transliterations."

The fact is that even if Herter Norton thought of herself as sticking to the German, she couldn't have produced "sensitively balanced," much less superbly readable, English if she actually had stuck to the German. She once described what she was doing as "using Rilke's own words and adhering to the rhythm of his prose," but that is misleading: she used English words and rhythm, and changed what needed changing. Elsewhere she wrote: "As you know, I have always believed that a simple, very close adherence to the original most justly conveys the quality of Rilke's style, and that his German and our English language are not so unrelated as to make this impossible." Yet her previous sentence called for "simple words, clarity, and typical rhythm"—not mentioning something her work proves she knew, namely that simplicity, clarity, and typicality are different in different languages.

By the usual standards of judging a translation, Herter Norton's work is very good: remarkably faithful as well as vigorous, tight, concise. Almost every passage of her prose translations, set alongside other versions, has fewer words and takes up less space. But more than just being concise or having "better" rhythm or word choice, her translations are defined by her vision of who Rilke is. For her, he is the canonical Great Man, one who speaks to us all. Her translator's note to *Letters to a Young Poet*, the first page of text in her edition, frames Rilke as follows: "It is evident that a great artist, whatever the immediate conditions disturbing his own life, may be able to clarify for the benefit of another those fundamental truths the conviction of which lies too deep in his consciousness to be reached by external agitations." In general, the fact that Rilke wrote his letters of advice and consolation in his twenties doesn't mean in Herter Norton's view that they were young and immature, for his mature great spirit was always speaking through him: throughout his life "the legend of the weary poet is dispelled, and in the end we find him always young, always constructive, the eminently positive philosopher of these letters." Her *Letters to a Young Poet* sounds different from other translations not least because her Rilke is more monumental than theirs.

In judging a translation, then, the ideal of "faithfulness" is an empty tautology: we are really judging what the translator sees in the author or text and chooses to be faithful to. At least in the case of good or decent translators. Some translators simply can't see what's there or can't re-create it—can't make their jokes funny, can't set the lyrical parts singing, or just misunderstand what the book says—and it makes sense to condemn those translations as unfaithful. But more often than not, the problem even there is a failure to see, to read well enough.

Since whether a translation works depends on the publication's genre and purpose as well as the translator's goals and understanding of their own position in the publishing world and the world at large, I generally respect translations on their own terms, even if they're not for me. But I do sometimes run across translations that make me genuinely angry. While I think my judgments of them are fair, my anger must be due to their representing what I most reject, what I most don't want my own translating and writing to be—so they are worth discussing as a kind of photographic negative of my commitments.

Some of the translations of Walter Benjamin in the four-volume selection of his writings, for instance, clearly do what they set out to do, but what they set out to do is make the opening sentence of his important and beautiful essay on Goethe's novel of love *Elective Affinities* sound like this:

> The writings we have on works of literature suggest that the
> minuteness of the detail in such studies be reckoned more to
> the account of the interests of philology than critique.[5]

5. Walter Benjamin, *Selected Writings*, vol. 1, *1913–1926*, ed. Marcus Bullock and Michael W. Jennings (Belknap Press of Harvard University Press, 1996),

This isn't "Pull back, Baboon's penis! . . . Horus's glide path—
TWICE," but it's close. Reading Benjamin in the original
doesn't feel like being repeatedly hit on the head, and reading
him in translation shouldn't either. The translator here, who
shall remain nameless, has left the nouns as nouns, complete
with suffixes that are weak in English ("the minuteness of the
detail," not "minute detail," or omitting the pleonasm altogether by using a genuine English noun such as "minutiae" or
"specificity"). "Writings" and "literature," much less "writings"
and "works of literature," form a sharp enough contrast in
German (*Literatur* vs. *Dichtungen*) but not in English, especially right at the start. The idiom *auf Rechnung setzen* has been
translated literally, with a cognate shoehorned in as an extra
word—"reckon to the account of" (*Rechnung*, "a calculation"
or "an account," is cognate with "reckon")—yet "the account
of the interests" makes no sense in English, whether or not as
something a minuteness can be reckoned to. The "interests of
philology" and "interests of critique," aside from the rest, also
make less sense in English than in German: we talk about "pursuing the *goals* of" a discipline or practice, not about that discipline or practice having *interests*. Anyway, if it seems important
to keep the accounting metaphor, then "reckoned more to the
account of the interests of" could instead be "chalked up to"

---

p. 297. The German is "*Die vorliegende Literatur über Dichtungen legt es nahe, Aus-
führlichkeit in dergleichen Untersuchungen mehr auf Rechnung eines philologischen
als eines kritischen Interesses zu setzen.*"

X rather than Y. We're not done yet: the word "philology" refers to something different in the German context (closer to
literary analysis in general, not etymology or narrow linguistic
parsing), as do "critique" and "criticism"; "critical" in English,
unless yoked to certain nouns as in "critical theory," strongly
connotes "crucially important" or "disparaging, judgmental"
more than the German *kritisch* does.

Overall, Benjamin is saying something like: "Studies
of novels and poems tend to try to be as detailed as possible, and to use this detail in the service of explication, not
critical analysis." Not only does this sentence actually mean
something, unlike "The writings we have on works of literature suggest that the minuteness of the detail in such studies
be reckoned more to the account of the interests of philology than critique," it functions to invite readers into a wide-
ranging and insightful essay, not make them run screaming
from the sixty more pages to go.

This translation makes me angry because I can't help it
feeling to me like a lack of care or, ultimately, love. Why, I
ask myself, does this translator think it is all right to make
Walter Benjamin sound like this? Does he not think Benjamin
would mind? Why does he have no problem inflicting such
miserable, impenetrable prose on the non-German-speaking
students of literature or philosophy who will have to read it?
Does he hate them for not knowing German? Does he resent
the prospect of anyone having easier access to Benjamin's
ideas than he had? My anger extends to the editors of the

volume, the expert readers who vetted it, the blurbers who praised it. Why did no one care enough stop this?[6]

It is as clear to me as to anyone else that these reactions are unfair; I am sure that the translator in question, not to mention everyone else involved in the publication, is a perfectly decent person who intended no harm to his students or to Walter Benjamin. He was working in a genre of academic philosophy translation where this sort of sentence is suitable, and the rules of that genre are not his fault. Still, I am confessing my emotions here, over the top though they are, because they define, in sharp inverse form, what I think a translation should be: Attentive to how the translating language works, overriding any demand for "equivalence" with how the original language works. Keeping in mind and keeping to heart the interests of readers, the author, and the author's ideas. (This, by the way, is how we use the word "interests" in English.) Feeling some responsibility to enable, or at the very least try to enable, the original author and their new readers to interact with one another at their respective best. An act of care, and ultimately love.

But I can't honestly say that the translation of this sentence I gave three paragraphs ago is more faithful than the published one. All translators are faithful, but to different things: to

6. As my book went to press, I learned of a new retranslation of Benjamin's essay forthcoming in *Walter Benjamin: Writings on Goethe*, translated by Susan Bernstein, Peter Fenves, and Kevin McLaughlin (Stanford University Press). I am happy to report that the translation there is clear and good, and I can stop leaping to Walter Benjamin's defense now; their version of the first sentence is: "The existing writings on literary works suggest that the level of detail in such investigations owes more to philological than to critical interest."

whatever they feel is most important to preserve. What's most important to preserve in a given translation, as well as how to go about preserving it, depends partly on the publishing context: is it an academic monograph, a textbook for language learners, a popular trade book with no footnotes? Those contexts will demand different kinds of fidelity. More fundamentally, though, what's important to preserve depends on what the translator finds in the original—how the translator reads. Everyone thinks, just as Herter Norton does, that they're "following the original," but they're working from different originals: each is trying to produce a text that matches, or does the same as (has the same force as), not the source text but *his or her reading of the source text*. Even the least literal translations, the most wildly divergent "imitations" or "reimaginings," try to stay true to whatever ineffable aspect of the original's vibe the writer of the new version feels they are taking up. That is why there is no objectively best translation, one that is "closest" to "the" original, as talk about faithfulness falsely implies.[7] We never say a reading is faithful or

7. Karen Emmerich's *Literary Translation and the Making of Originals* (Bloomsbury, 2017) argues along multiple lines that original texts are made, not born: constituted from unstable sources in the process of pinning down whatever it is we are going to translate from, whether this means selecting an authoritative edition, creating an ideal edition by incorporating variations from other versions (often justified as discerning the author's true intentions, even if they never all appeared in the same single text), or more aggressively constructing the text altogether, in the cases of fragmentary or ancient works like the *Epic of Gilgamesh*. The decision about what to translate in the first place ascribes value, defines boundaries, and shapes the canon of both the translating language/community and the source. But even if there were a fixed, stable original—or even after we have come to a consensus about what text to take as our original—every translator is still going to read it differently.

unfaithful, because we realize that a reading is a response, not a copy. Each translator translates a different thing, in precisely the same way that each reader of a given book reads a different book, and yet, in another way, not.

Here we have, perhaps unexpectedly, the most far-reaching consequence of understanding translation as a kind of reading: no one translates a text—they translate their reading of the text, and everyone has different reading experiences (different from other readers', different over time). The ideal of fidelity presupposes a certain fixity—not unlike the fixed constellations of stars in the sky—while translation as reading makes us insist on the translator as an individual in an interpersonal, social, political world, someone with personal tastes and a history and more or less power than other people and communities, and makes us consider translation an act performed in this specific lived context. Trying to define the best way to translate is like trying to define how an actor in a movie should put on a jacket.[8]

I said just now that judging a translation by how faithful it is is an empty tautology, but in practice, of course, translations

8. I take this simile from a comment by the director Billy Wilder in Cameron Crowe, *Conversations with Wilder* (Knopf, 1999), who I thought said you could tell how truly great an actor Cary Grant was simply by how he put on a jacket. But I find I have misremembered. Wilder does say that Grant—like Tom Cruise— "makes the hard things look simple. On film, Cary Grant could walk into the room and say 'Tennis anyone?' like no one else. You don't value the skill until you see a less skilled actor try the same thing. It's gold." The jacket comes in a later discussion, of Tom Cruise in *Rain Man* even though Dustin Hoffman got the praise: the real task of acting is to "just open a drawer beautifully and take out a tie and put on a jacket," though the Oscars "don't notice the guy who does all the hard work, who is making it look easy"—they reward the actors who play flashy, histrionic, superficially difficult roles (pp. 6, 14).

are judged as faithful or unfaithful all the time—by prospective publishers, reviewers, prize panels, tenure committees. Like any other practice that, in theory, doesn't have to be a certain way but in reality is the way it is (correct spelling, appropriate behavior in a job interview, tailoring a jacket), the practice of producing and praising faithful translations can be looked at sociologically, as one way among others to navigate the real-world social structures and power dynamics we find ourselves in.

If we argue for—or take for granted—the commonsensical ideal of fidelity as a criterion of good translation, then our producing such a translation will be an act of, among other things, proving our scholarly or philological skills (and implicitly reinforcing the need for and value of such skills); taking our place in a community of experts (as proved by positive peer reviews or editorial judgments, by critics with the proper standards writing in the proper venues, by tenure committees, etc.); presenting ourself as an expert vis-à-vis the lay public of readers who will experience the text only in translation; casting the original text as an object of reverence, which needs and deserves to be respected and transmitted faithfully to receptive readers in the translating language, as unchanged as possible, unless merely enhanced with footnotes and introductions; above all, avoiding the negative qualities of "bad" translations: clumsiness, excess, lack of balance and harmony, anything unsavory or kitschy, letting oneself be contaminated or corrupted by the other language or text (translationese, amorality, letting another's voice "infect" or "penetrate" you more generally), and, most alarmingly, the irresponsible hoax of claiming that something is really in the original when in fact it comes merely from the translator. These are all more or less my intentions as a translator too. But they are not the only goals it is possible to have. Rather than take them for granted, as many translators, reviewers, editors, and scholars would, it is fairer to treat them as just one possible approach to our public, political, professional situation—and a relatively conformist, conservative, non-boat-rocking approach at that.

Ultimately, what we are doing is reasserting our claim to belong within the boundaries of a language community. This is Naoki Sakai's argument, in his 2009 essay "How Do We Count a Language? Translation and Discontinuity,"[9] which he introduces by saying that there are never simply "borders" but always "bordering": constitutive acts of defining the border between included and excluded. The lines of acceptability are constantly being drawn and policed; we are constantly reminded that we are accepted into a community *if and only if* we conduct ourselves properly (that is, continue to conduct ourselves properly). When it comes to language, there are no safely ensconced, guaranteed insiders—in the community of English speakers, of Americans, of "Western civilization"—only a constant process of speaking, writing, and behaving in suitable ways to prove that we

9. *Translation Studies* 2.1 (2009): 71–88; in more detail in Sakai, *Voices of the Past: The Status of Language in Eighteenth-Century Japanese Discourse* (Cornell University Press, 1992).

belong, or else of resisting our inclusion, or demonstrating our unfitness for membership in the community as judged by its other members.

The conclusion about translation which Sakai draws from this premise is that both "source languages" and "target languages" are constituted or defined after the fact, by the fact, of translation. After all, if we fully accept that people exist in hybrid, diverse language communities, as I argued in chapter 2— that translators realign texts to reach different audiences already within their communities—then there is no firm segregation between languages, between speakers of different languages, to begin with. A source language defined as different from a target language doesn't exist until there is a translator to whom it is comprehensible and an audience to whom it is incomprehensible; the translator is someone in an ambiguous position within an already heterogeneous community, whose ambiguity defines two "sides" of a division. Translation is not the ferrying of preexisting meaning across a gap but a retroactive creation of meaning ("in" the "other language") out of non-sense (the incomprehensibility of the source before the act of translation took place). In short, translation is an act of "bordering," creating sense on what is now represented as "both sides" of a language gap.

If we don't do this properly, we are judged to be bad translators. My list above of the qualities of "bad translations"— clumsy, kitschy, corrupted, and so on—is taken from the translator and theorist Johannes Göransson, who welcomes such destabilizing forces and resolutely focuses on aspects of translations besides their fidelity. For him, poetry is not an object of placid contemplation but a "deformation zone" (à la Shklovsky), upending our expectations and lives, deregulating and deranging, violent and volatile. While Rilke describes the poem as a constellation, unusable and lasting—prompting an aesthetic response of distanced, quasi-visual appreciation— Göransson talks about a poem's effects differently, in a tradition which includes Emily Dickinson saying that poetry takes the top of her head off, Kafka saying that it is an ax blow to the frozen sea within us. Whereas traditional theorists of translation and ideal communication—Göransson's example is George Steiner in *After Babel*—generally aim to fight off or forestall the various risks of "bad translation" in favor of the calm, supremely manageable results of smooth and expert fidelity, Göransson counters: "Where [Steiner] sees threat, I see promise."[10] He rejects entirely the implicit standard of mastery that lies behind the ideal of faithful translation—the expertise needed to produce, evaluate, and appreciate a translation's fidelity: "Poetry is not meant to be mastered," he writes in his book's last paragraph. "It is meant to draw us into its foreign orbits."

And there are other ways we might champion different standards of value besides fidelity (or infidelity). Madhu H. Kaza evokes translation as "an act of hospitality . . . conceived

---

10. Johannes Göransson, *Transgressive Circulation: Essays on Translation* (Noemi, 2018), p. 33, building on Joyelle McSweeney and Johannes Göransson, *Deformation Zone* (Ugly Duckling, 2012).

not as charity, not as condescension or even merely tolerance," but as inviting a guest, his or her dignity honored, to join us at our kitchen table.[11] The ethical task of welcoming someone new into the community extends to translators too: Kaza is less concerned with judging a translation as good or bad than she is with encouraging those who might not feel welcomed into the profession to try translating in the first place. Many interpreters and translators of less literary texts, such as courtroom testimony,[12] emphasize the body: the way "translation is not just about transposing words from one language to another. But transplanting a feeling, a way of seeing the world, from one vocabulary of experience to another. . . . To translate a text is to enter into the most intimate relationship with it possible. It is the translator's body, almost more so than the translator's mind, that is the vessel of transfer."[13] It would be possible to redescribe this transference in terms of faithful translation (i.e., a good translation is "faithful" to the author's way of seeing the world, not to literal verbal accuracy), but I would describe respect for others' experiences as different than privileging fidelity to the foreign text, though they are

11. Editor's note to *Kitchen Table Translation*, special issue, *Aster(ix) Journal* (Summer 2017): 12–17.

12. Antena [Jen Hofer and John Pluecker], *A Manifesto for Interpretation as Instigation / Un manifiesto para la interpretación como instigación* (2013), downloadable at https://antenaantena.org/wp-content/uploads/2012/06/interpasinstig.pdf.

13. Lina Mounzer, "War in Translation," in *Kitchen Table Translation*, pp. 137, 139.

comparable approaches to navigating the task of translation. The philosophical framework I have presented in this book encompasses both of these two approaches equally—it just depends how you see the action and "force" of an utterance. I said at the start of this chapter that moving away from the ideal of "faithful translation"—or recasting it as one way among others of navigating a complex social world—involves emphasizing the personal role of the translator. This includes both the body of the translator and, more or less explicitly, the political context of that body. From colonial powers banning the use of indigenous languages, to job applicants judged for class markers in their speech or uptalk, vocal fry, and other female speech patterns; from linguistically closed communities where certain religious texts might be taboo in the original language and sacrilegious to translate, to political contexts of differing access to political or legal rights depending on language, languages are deeply tied to individual lives and also to the wider nation, tribe, or community of speakers. As we know from the German Romantic ideas of language discussed in chapter 1, the bond between language and individual is at the same time a bond between language and community, and so the use of language is always a social and political act.

We can emphasize the social context more or less explicitly. The description above of translating testimony as an intimate, bodily personal relationship with someone else's experience comes from Lina Mounzer's explicitly political essay "War in Translation," while Madhu Kaza describes the context of her translation work in terms of personal loss, largely leaving aside the wider political reasons for her childhood experience: "Translation from my first language, Telugu, is actually quite painful for me. (I enjoy translating from other languages.) It's painful because I'm constantly reminded of loss. I was brought to the US when I was five, and mostly stopped speaking my first language. That language is a love of my life . . . and it feels very far away from me most days. I do translation from Telugu as a way of reckoning with that loss. . . . Translation for me is repair work."[14] Don Mee Choi, on the other hand, puts national politics front and center, emphasizing the wider sociopolitical experience of domination that made her personal experience of multilingual life painful: "I come from a land where we are taught that the US saved us from Commies and that North Korea is our enemy. I come from a land of neocolonial fratricide." In that context, "I am not content to just go from Korean to English. I am not content to uphold the notion of national literature—the notion that literature outside of the Western canon is always bound to national borders." She refuses to treat Korean and English as parallel, comparable languages, because they "are misaligned by neocolonial war, militarism, and neoliberal economy." In her case too, though, this power relation is embedded in her own person: she says her language has always been foreign, "a site of power takeover, war, wound, deformation, and, ultimately and already, motherless"; later she writes, "As foreign

14. "How Do You Want to Be Wrong? Talking with Madhu H. Kaza," https://therumpus.net/2018/05/14/the-rumpus-interview-with-madhu-h-kaza/.

words myself, I seek incomprehensibility—a mirror image of myself." Elsewhere, explicitly equating national and personal power imbalances, she writes: "My translational intent has nothing to do with personal growth, intellectual exercise, or cultural exchange, which implies an equal standing of some sort. South Korea and the U.S. are not equal. I am not transnationally equal."[15] All these different writers on translation insist, differently, on understanding translation practice as grounded in the individual translator, while at the same time the individual translator is grounded in wider sociopolitical contexts.

With these issues in mind, we can realize that an apolitical aesthetic realm of literary translation is simply another political context, available to translators who claim that kind of position. In my own work, and in the examples I've given in earlier chapters in this book, the stakes are arguably not especially high: if we fail to take account of some element of

15. The Choi quotations are from her *Translation Is a Mode = Translation Is an Anti-neocolonial Mode* (Ugly Duckling Presse, 2020), based on a keynote lecture at the 2016 American Literary Translators Association conference in Oakland, CA, except for the last, which Daniel Borzutzky used as the epigraph for an essay on his own fraught linguistic position (*Memories of My Overdevelopment* [Kenning Editions, 2015]). Like Choi, Borzutzky emphasizes wider political dynamics as the necessary context for his own personal history: he describes himself as having been forced to flee Chile with his family due to the murderous austerity policies and repressive violence developed by the economists known as "the Chicago Boys," while now he is living and working in Chicago under murderous austerity policies and repressive violence reimported from Chile. If, as he argues in one poem, "Chicago is a Chilean city"—if the various "devouring economies" of different nations are "borderless"—then what does it mean to translate between Spanish and English?

the force of a text, if we translate some aspect of German too literally or not literally enough, we have produced an aesthetically mediocre or bad translation, but it's not like anyone gets hurt. This is the experience of translation in a rarefied space of literature as artistic pursuit. But if Telugu or Korean is not a neutral choice of language for Kaza or Choi, then my German and French were not neutral choices either, even if they have been made to feel that way. Decades ago, in my New York City middle school, the four options for my language requirement were Latin, French, German, and Spanish: I took Latin, and internalized in ways I never truly appreciated the ideology that German and French were Important Major Languages while others—Korean, Russian—weren't. Kaza describes the "sad history" of her futile, decades-long efforts to find a way to learn Telugu as an adult; the lack of classes, teachers, funding, and other opportunities that she encountered was not arbitrary or coincidental but structural.[16] Nowadays, judging from the schools my son's education has exposed me to, the Important Major Languages on the menu in the US are Spanish and Mandarin—the status or power of China has gone up, that of Western Europe has gone down, with Spanish being predominantly seen in this context as a language of the Americas, no

---

16. Madhu H. Kaza, "Not a Good Fit," in *Violent Phenomena: 21 Essays on Translation*, ed. Kavita Bhanot and Jeremy Tiang (Tilted Axis, 2022), p. 310. As it were objectively—from an abstract, purely apolitical perspective that does not actually exist—there is no reason why Telugu should not be widely taught in America: "Though few people in the U.S. have heard of it, Telugu is not obscure. It is a major language, with over 80 million speakers worldwide, one of the top fifteen languages spoken in the world and the fastest growing language in the U.S."

less than English, despite their linguistic homelands across the Atlantic. Korean and Russian are still not options.

Kaza at one point describes her idea of people like me as follows: "For a long time I thought of translators as those white Americans who grow up monolingual and who take a random German or Japanese class in college, say, or read Nouveaux Romans or Latin American Boom fiction and get inspired, and pursue the language and years later become translators. I am amazed at the confident, progressive, relatively linear—even if slow—trajectories of those stories. These stories fit with Western ideas of mastery," and "I don't think of 'mastery' as the same thing as 'excellence.' Mastery can coincide with a discourse of domination." The language of "coinciding" is a sharp way to put it: irrespective of how much domination someone consciously or intentionally tries to exert, their trajectory can coincide with domination. Those German classes used resources that didn't go into offering Russian or Telugu classes and ended up endowing me with kinds of prestige that I could leverage into book deals to translate from languages that US editors are more receptive to, or possibly prizes, or the ability to publish a book like this one; in addition to these positive advantages, I enjoyed the negative ones of, for instance, not feeling loss or pain when translating from any of the languages I translate, and not having been colonized like Choi and her language community.

Then again, even Kaza's placid, confident white US American choosing a language that the culture views as prestigious is doubtless driven by personal forces as well. (Why German, not Spanish or French? Why learn a foreign language at all, not banking or basketball or busking, never mind becoming Rilke's carpenter, cobbler, or cooper?) There are certainly losses and psychic needs in my own life that are more or less thoroughly sublimated into my work as a translator—I even know what some of them are.

My overall point, and the lesson of the philosophy I've presented in this book, is that it doesn't come down to the translator's identity—it comes down to how we navigate that identity through the social and interpersonal world around us. Kaza describes translating Spanish as pleasant, unfraught, and relatively nonbodily, much as I would describe translating German—in other words, the path she describes for those white Americans is a path she is on too. For someone else, Spanish can be just as fraught as Telugu is and Spanish isn't for her: Urayoán Noel, a poet and translator originally from Puerto Rico, describes having "the *conciencia*, being Puerto Rican, that language is colonial and racialized and classed in all these ways. And I think I bring that to whatever I do." That is to say, a Spanish-to-English translator may embody international relationships more like Choi's Korean and English, although the historical relationships will always be particular—"as a Caribbean person translating a South American poet," Noel writes, he is "thinking also about the different cadences of these different kinds of Spanish that reflect different histories of empire and conquest and migration and diaspora."[17]

17. "Violence, Beauty, Structure, Freedom: An Interview with Translator Urayoán Noel," https://www.asymptotejournal.com/blog/2022/03/09/violence-beauty-structure-freedom-an-interview-with-translator-urayoan-noel/.

My personal, relatively placid trajectory is to some extent an accident of birth and history, but also partly a choice: I could have decided to learn and translate from Yiddish, steeped in the erasures of Yiddish speakers and Yiddish culture from mid-twentieth-century Europe and then New York City; I could have decided to champion and translate writing in Native American languages from past and present; I could have run across something that made me decide I wanted to learn Telugu, and then faced the challenges Kaza describes. There are any number of paths I didn't take and thus relations between English and other languages that didn't shape me.

In terms of conceptualizing the political relationships among various languages, the best historical work I know of is Alexander Beecroft's *An Ecology of World Literature*.[18] After basing his "ecological" metaphor in some detail on the ecozones, biomes, and ecoregions of our actual planetary environment, he lays out six types of ecology and the ways in which languages and literatures within each interact with one another, as well as how one ecology develops into another. The crucial ecology today is the national one, resting on the post–German Romantic linkages among a people, a language, a nation, and a state (hence a "national language" is different from a vernacular language even if it emerged from one, and

18. *An Ecology of World Literature: From Antiquity to the Present Day* (Verso, 2015), esp. pp. 1–36, 203–205, 229–230, 235–241. A more personal book, from a creative writer's perspective, that covers much the same ground is Minae Mizumura, *The Fall of Language in the Age of English*, tr. Mari Yoshihara and Juliet Winters Carpenter (Columbia, 2015).

is also different from the emerging, not fully realized "global" ecology of literature).

In a national ecology, national literary histories arise, establishing canonical works central to the language and culture (even if those texts are prenational, e.g., *Beowulf*) while texts that can't be integrated into the reigning nationalist narrative are marginalized (not every novel written within the geographical boundaries of the United States counts as a work of "American literature"—especially if not in English). Literary/cultural values that emerged in one nation are exported and imposed as universal values wherever possible. There tends to be either universalization and appropriation, or exoticization and exclusion, both within the sphere of a given national language and in its interactions with other languages that are thereby truly either "domesticated" or "foreignized."

The way to avoid these destructive patterns of cross-cultural interaction, even when works are imagined as rooted in a single national language, is to recognize the complexity and "dialogism" within each side. Cross-cultural comparisons, Beecroft writes, tend to cast each culture as more homogeneous than it truly is, reducing each side "to a monologic and hegemonic narrative, whose interactions with the monologic narratives of other cultures can in turn be reduced either to exoticism or to universalism." His example is of the encounter between the Chinese concept of *wenxue* (文学, originally referring, in a Confucian context, to "the learning and knowledge associated with canonical written texts") and the Western concept of "literature," which entered China in the nineteenth century and started to be translated as *wenxue*. One way to describe what happened is as "a simple and familiar story of the erosion of indigenous concepts in subaltern cultures replaced by terms borrowed from hegemonic European cultures," but in fact, by focusing on the debates about "literature" in eighteenth- and nineteenth-century Europe (resulting in a new definition where literature is "imaginative textuality, including poetry, drama, and prose fiction but excluding philosophy, history, and science"), as well as debates in China at the time (e.g., about whether philosophy and history are literary), we can "recuperate this exercise in cultural translation as something other than a simple act of cultural imperialism and/or appropriation." Like the contexts of a Cuban novel and the American readers falsely imagined as entirely monolingual and monocultural, Beecroft writes that "there is a tendency to imagine both Europe and China as static and monologic cultural entities . . . the assumption seems to be that the dialogism of each internal cultural debate is put aside during moments of translation." Sometimes, the imperialism and appropriation that seem to have taken place are more artifacts of the later literary historian than truly part of the crosslinguistic interaction.

But Beecroft's account does leave something out about the interaction between languages and literatures inside this national ecology and those outside—across the kind of power differential described and inhabited by Choi. He is admirably concrete and clear about how, for instance, the national ecology provides a relatively limited number of "slots" for the

most-favored nations with national literatures, while works
from elsewhere get lumped into regions ("African" literature,
"Arabic" literature, "Francophone" literature . . . even novels
that could not be more explicitly grounded in their respective
nation's history—*One Hundred Years of Solitude* or *Midnight's
Children*—get received as works of "Latin American literature"
or "postcolonial fiction"). But he is describing the situation
firmly as seen from *within* the national ecology. Any system
of literary value, Beecroft argues, necessarily excludes, draws
boundaries, and reduces information—its goal, in a sense, is
to "reduce canons to manageable proportions by identify-
ing entire categories of literature that can be ignored and by
establishing criteria for evaluating what remains." He knows
that these exclusions are always political, but "in the end," he
writes, since "the sheer volume of literary production" requires *some* kind of reduction, "no literary ecology . . . should
be disparaged simply because some form of literary production fails to be viable within it; that much is unavoidable."

Inevitable dynamic or not, the people writing in languages
excluded from the national-literature ecology, or interacting
with the center from the periphery by translating between
such languages and English, have something to say about it.
And in fact, while writers who do resist and "disparage" this
dynamic, such as Don Mee Choi and Urayoán Noel, might
seem to be exceptions—more precisely: although the system
of nationhood and national literatures is set up to categorize
them as exceptions—they are actually the rule. You might
say that the difference is not between those within a power

structure and those outside it but between those made to think they are not required to negotiate that power structure and those who negotiate it more consciously.

Like any interaction with forces outside oneself, translation can be either a subjection to others' authority or an exertion of one's own power, or both, and since we are never in an isolated, Adamic state of pure freedom to begin with, any new force will either strengthen or resist the forces we are already subject to. There is no way to know once and for all whether we are being changed by something new or imposing ourselves on it—and no way to anticipate once and for all whether being changed will be welcome or oppressive. Translation is not necessarily glorious bridge building, though it can be, nor necessarily hegemonic appropriation, though it can be. Even when we are just being exposed to something new, from a Rilke poem to the meanings of Native American names to the glossaries in the backs of translations of Arabic novels, it remains up for debate and grabs whether we are curious about these new bits of language and cultural reference for good reasons or bad, genuinely interested or obnoxiously exoticizing. The languages I've learned have certainly opened up horizons and experiences in my life, while also coinciding with the closing off or exclusion of other horizons and experiences. It will always be both, because even new ways of looking at the world are at the same time the absence of still other new ways of looking at the world.

Translation thus shares fully in all the complex ethical dilemmas raised by our dealings with other people. It doesn't solve those problems, nor in my view does it raise any especially original version of the problems we find in any line of work or way of life. The issue of representation in translation, for instance—the importance of publishing more translations from the Arab world or Africa or foreign genre fiction—seems to me not especially different from other crucial issues of representation in publishing, such as the importance of having Black or Asian American or Native American or queer or women's voices in English-language publications, editorial offices, and prize committees. Except insofar as every individual case is different, which it is. People act and say things and prompt responses, and the ethics of how to respond appropriately are complex, in translation just as with any other move we make in the world.

8

CODA

"Poetry is what gets lost in translation." What does this mean? I think the first-blush interpretation is "The true poetry of something lies beyond words. Translation can translate words, but not what the original ineffably conveys." This actually makes no sense, because if the "poetry" of a poem is its non-verbal core or heart or depth or True Meaning—its Platonic "Idea"—then the poem's original language has no connection to it either, and whether you put the words into French or Chinese or Anishinaabe or English, those new words will have the same ability to convey the idea as the original words, that is, none.

What Frost's slogan must mean—and he's right—is that "poetry" is in the relation or connection between word and essence, the evoking or conveying of the Idea *by* the language. Since poetry is something words do, that particular poetry is lost when all of the words are changed. It is equally true, though, that poetry gets created in translation, for the new words in the new language are in a new relationship with the Idea, and they convey whatever they convey in a new way, within a new linguistic system and for a new audience. "Poetry is what gets lost when someone other than the author reads a poem"; "Poetry is what gets created when someone other than the author reads a poem." These are equally true as well, and for the same reason.

"Poetry is what gets gained in translation": may writers of newspaper headlines and posters to Pinterest someday be as obsessed with this new slogan as they are with the Frost line!

Nowadays, the more burning question seems to be whether or not poetry is what gets lost in ChatGPT. Once again, artificial intelligence and whether or not it will replace the human writer is a hot topic—as it was some years ago too, when Google Translate was starting to get more reliable, a process that continues.[1] But while Google Translate is relevant to translation, ChatGPT is not, for a reason that reveals something deep about its limitations.

You can ask ChatGPT to "write a story in the style of Marcel Proust," but that is different from "Translate this particular Proust story into English": the latter is precisely what ChatGPT can't do, because to translate a story requires

---

1. See for instance David Bellos, "I, Translator," *New York Times*, March 21, 2010; Esther Allen, "Can Google Help Translate a Classic Novel?," *Publishers Weekly*, August 26, 2016, which contains the *barco* example discussed below.

reading it. Translation is a kind of writing linked to a kind of reading—a reading of another text, the original. While Chat-GPT can comb and cull and copy and crib and collage—and to that extent it can "write"—what it can't do is read. This is why it generates references to nonexistent legal precedents and fake articles, quotes passages that aren't real, and so on: it is fed with and works with texts, rather than coming into contact with what's actually in the world.

Translation reveals, in other words, that when we talk about "the deeply human enterprise" of creativity or thought that ChatGPT cannot replace, what we're really talking about is the deeply human act of reading: the process, subjective and objective at once, of engaging as an individual person with something that exists out there in shared reality.

As for Google Translate and other translation AI, I am as fascinated as anyone else by the impressive technological magic of such programs; I am grateful for being able to read websites in other languages, point my phone at wall text in a museum in another country and get a good amount of the information it contains, and so forth. As a citizen, I am concerned by the labor issue of artificial intelligence combing the world for work by writers and translators and then appropriating it without credit or payment. But as a translator I find talk of the existential threat posed to my career completely pointless.

In effect, Google Translate is the same kind of tool as a bilingual dictionary. I could stand at that wall text in the museum with a Spanish-English dictionary and look up all the words, maybe refer to a Spanish grammar book written for English speakers, and in half an hour or so I would get a good amount of the information that the wall text contains. (I wouldn't be able to do this with Chinese or Arabic text, of course.) If I point my phone and tap the screen, Google Translate will as it were look up all the words at once and provide English counterparts in something like the right grammatical relationships. (It doesn't literally work by using dictionaries in this way, but that is the effect.) This is undoubtedly more efficient, but no more threatening to my job or my humanity than a dictionary.

The program may have access to every possible meaning out there, but it cannot reliably choose among them. Even stock phrases and clichés are no help when they don't align across languages: Esther Allen gives the example of Google Translate invariably converting the Spanish *barco* into "boat," unable to consider the English expression "When my ship comes in" because in Spanish that is the more biblical, less mercantile *Cuando lleguen las vacas gordas*, "When the fat cattle come." No ships. *Barco* therefore never summons up the phrase, even though a character awaiting a *barco* with desperate longing should in English be waiting for a "ship" to come in, not a "boat," to activate this association. In general, although Google Translate makes different characteristic mistakes in each of the language pairs I have experimented with, I have noticed particular problems with languages where the same word means many different things in the language being translated into. *Baguettes* in French means baguettes, drumsticks, chopsticks . . . The word will be translated correctly in close proximity to words about a bakery, a drum set, or Chinese food; the program can't otherwise use common sense about the context, because it has none.

More fundamental than glitches of word choice is the fact that AI is incapable of producing utterances—it can produce only words and sentences. As Bakhtin rightly showed (see chapter 4), semantic and grammatical units mean nothing by themselves: they are not intended, inflected, given force until spoken or written in an utterance by an actual mind. Some kinds of statement are minimally inflected, produced with minimal human subjectivity behind them—hotel checkout times, digital camera instruction booklets, informational wall texts, most online listicles—and these can be effectively produced or indeed translated by artificial intelligence. I have described them as pieces of language with an "arrow" that can be redirected and practically no "arc" to be re-created. But any real utterance, which certainly includes anything in a work of literature, argument, or rhetoric, requires from the translator inflection and intentionality in its use of language. In short, a text run through AI translation still has to be translated.

Here are two examples taken more or less at random from an art history text I recently translated, by Anne Bertrand. In each example, the first passage in English is the original put through Google Translate in 2023, the second is my translation:

Des essais littéraires du jeune homme subsistent plusieurs textes courts, certains plutôt réussis, au point que l'on peut se demander comment il se fait qu'il n'ait pu parvenir à les faire publier.

Of the young man's literary essays there are several short texts, some quite successful, to the point that one wonders how it is that he could not manage to have them published.

Among the young man's literary efforts were several prose meditations good enough that it's surprising he couldn't get them published.

"Essais" does mean "essays," but it also means "attempts," "ventures," which of course is why Montaigne named his new genre of exploratory prose "essays." Here the context of literature makes the translation of *"essais"* as "essays" superficially plausible; in fact, a sensitive reader would realize that "literary essays" is redundant and that saying "there are several short texts among the essays" is pointless, so the noun must be different. The French *"textes,"* meanwhile, does mean "texts"; it was the translator's mind and knowledge of English conventions that made him decide "texts" was too vague and so sounded wrong here, and prompted him to query the author about which more specific noun—essays, stories, reviews, poems?—was correct in this case.

In the following example, the all-at-once dictionary gets each word pretty much correct but is unable to put the pieces of the sentence together in a way that makes sense in English:

Peu d'éléments subsistent quant aux tentatives de publication de l'apprenti écrivain et traducteur, alors que la littérature l'occupe encore largement, même s'il se met peu à peu à la photographie.

Few elements remain as to the attempts at publication of the apprentice writer and translator, while literature still largely occupied him, even if he gradually took up photography.

He continued to work primarily as an apprentice writer and translator, even while gradually turning to photography, but little survives of his attempts to get published.

"Elements" ("*éléments*") is not what we'd call cover letters and pieces of writing submitted for publication, and "occupied him" is a bit too literal for "*l'occupe*"—English wants people as active subjects of its verbs, so "he was busy with work" or "he worked" is better than "work occupied him"—but the main task of the translator of this sentence is to rearrange the order that the information comes in to fit the expectations of the English-language reader. The French opens with the state of the archive, moves to the nature of the documents in question and the man who produced them, then reminds us that this writer is the photographer we're reading a book about (Walker Evans); English, in contrast, puts the facts in chronological order: he wrote and translated, then he started photographing, then papers got lost. The French text isn't trying to do anything fancy or counterintuitive against the baseline of the French language, so the translation should conform just as smoothly to expected usage in English.

None of the issues in these two examples is difficult to handle, and several would never have come up if the text weren't put through Google Translate in the first place, but

these cases of translation in action show the kind of engagement with language that AI doesn't have. What we might call
overall "naturalness"—conformity to real readers' assumptions and expectations—along with any unnaturalness or deviation from this baseline, is what an actual translation has to
be sensitive to.

I have been struck, in writing this book, by how many different
metaphors there are for translation and how they are all true,
they just describe different things. The translator is "playing a
piece of music": when you listen to Glenn Gould playing Bach,
you are listening to Bach—how could you listen to Bach any
better?—even though you are also listening to Glenn Gould.
(The arrow is doubled.) That is, a translation is not a less valid
version of an original—it's how we get access to the original.
If, on the other hand, you want to emphasize the changes a
text undergoes in translation—every word is now in another
language—then you might say the translator is "arranging" a
piano piece for saxophone or symphony, so every note comes
out different, played by different instruments. Both of these
metaphors express real truths even though they're mutually
exclusive. In *Don Quixote*, translations are said, admittedly
by a not very reliable speaker, to be "like looking at Flemish
tapestries from the wrong side, for although the figures are
visible, they are covered by threads that obscure them, and
cannot be seen with the smoothness and color of the right
side"; a twelfth-century Chinese monk translating Buddhist
sutras gave his translating language, and his culture's textiles,

more credit: "Translating is like turning over a piece of bro-
cade: back & front both gorgeous, the left & right reversed."[2]
Over the course of this book, I have invoked the metaphor of
gerrymandering to highlight the implicit evaluative process
of the translator selecting what is most indispensable; the
metaphor of developing the photograph of the original text;
the metaphor of tuning a radio dial between too German and
too American to find the best signal. There are the hoary old
metaphors of carrying semantic cargo from a "source" to a
"target," or pouring wine from an old bottle into a new one,
or cloaking thought in a new linguistic garment; there is Margaret Sayers Peden's metaphor of melting the ice cube of an
original work and then refreezing it, resulting in functionally
equivalent cubes even though many or all of the water mol-
ecules will be different;[3] there is Walter Benjamin's description of the language of a translation enveloping its substance
like a royal robe,[4] or his more famous one of translation and
original as shards of the same shattered vessel, "fragments of a
greater language," which in being reassembled have to "match
one another in the smallest details, although they need not

2. Miguel de Cervantes, *Don Quixote*, tr. Edith Grossman (Ecco, 2003),
p. 873; Fayun, quoted in Wong May's afterword to *In the Same Light: 200 Poems
for Our Century; From the Migrants & Exiles of the Tang Dynasty* (Song Cave,
2022), p. 354.

3. Margaret Sayers Peden, "Building a Translation, The Reconstruction Business: Poem 145 of Sor Juana Inés de la Cruz," in *The Craft of Translation*, ed. John
Biguenet and Rainer Schulte (University of Chicago Press, 1989), p. 13.

4. Benjamin, "The Task of the Translator"; see Berman's exquisite explication
in *Age of Translation*, pp. 159–164.

be like one another." Michael Emmerich gives the image of the translator "as a ghost who haunts languages, cultures, and nations, existing in two worlds at once but belonging fully to neither";[5] Madhu Kaza evokes translation as an act of hospitality. Translation also seems to generate wonderful metaphors for other, related aspects of reading and writing, for instance Jennifer Croft's image of the oyster scrunching up into itself, kabalistically leaving a little room for the microsuspense of any piece of language.[6] Everyone who has written about translation has their own favorite images; the list goes on and on, even before we get to the fiction writers with prominent translator characters (Alameddine, Bachmann, Cortázar . . .), the writer-translators for whom the two practices are close to inseparable (Borges, Anne Carson . . .), and all the other creative writers with what I think of as a translator's imagination.

I have come to feel that there are endless metaphors for translation because the process of translation and that of creating a metaphor are the same. Latin *trans-latio* is the same as Greek *meta-phora*, "over/beyond" + "bring or carry": *metaphora*, like *translatio*, also means "transportation" or "conveyance." And here we have another metaphor, another translation! In Greece, moving vans and long-distance cargo trucks are blazoned with the word ΜΕΤΑΦΟΡΑΙ: "Transport," but "Metaphors." Bringing a word or idea from the semantic zone it started off in to one where it is new and un-

---

5. Emmerich, "Beyond, Between," p. 50.
6. Croft, "Order of Things."

familiar is, equally, the act that creates the spark of a metaphor and the act that performs the "bordering" (Naoki Sakai's term) of any translation.

Yet all these proliferating metaphors are somehow unsatisfying. If anything can be "translation" and translation can be anything, then what's the point? Beyond the specific rhetorical context of using a metaphor—for instance, using the Glenn Gould metaphor to say that translations don't merely give partial, lesser access to the original—what does it really tell us? When I'm sitting down to translate, there are no metaphors. Those are just for interviews, or for talking with people about what translators do.

When I'm translating, I'm just reading—trying to pick up on as much as I can of the original utterance, its meaning and sound and allusions and tone and point of view and emotional impact. As I register what I feel is most important and indispensable, I try to write that indispensable thing in English; then, in revising, I reactivate the reading part of my mind and try to anticipate as much as I can of what an English-language reader with no access to the original will pick up on. Will something sound wrong, or remind them of something inappropriate, or be funny or unfunny; will they be able to read my translation as fully and richly, for the same sounds and meanings and feelings, as I was able to read the original? Or will "Brage" distract them by rhyming with "page"? Translation as an activity is an endlessly entertaining and illuminating way to engage with a text, and translations as end products give readers the chance to experience that same engagement, just as reading any other book lets a reader share with the author the fruitful miracle of communication. Nothing more than that, and nothing less.

ACKNOWLEDGMENTS

This book is the product of many years of working on translations and thinking about translation, and would not have been possible without all the editors, publishers, readers, writers, friends, and colleagues I have been lucky enough to read and talk things over with. My thanks to them all.

Some of *The Philosophy of Translation* draws directly on pieces I've written for various venues over the years, and I would like to thank in particular the editors who helped me write them: Donald Breckenridge at *The Brooklyn Rail*, Edwin Frank at New York Review Books Classics, Dan Piepenbring at The Paris Review Daily, Bob Weil and Pete Simon at W. W. Norton/ Liveright. Thanks also to Peter Cole for inviting me to give a lecture at Yale in 2021 that prompted me to pull together much of what became chapter 3. Among the living authors I translate, three have been especially enlightening to talk to about translation: Saša Stanišić, Victoria Kielland, and Jon Fosse.

I finished writing the book with the help of a Robert B. Silvers Grant for Works in Progress, which I gratefully acknowledge; my gratitude as well to all the organizations that have supported my translation work in the past: the National Endowment for the Arts, the Cullman Center at the New York Public Library, the Guggenheim Foundation, the Goethe Institute, the New York State Council of the Arts, the Foundation for Dutch Literature (NLPVF), the Peter Suhrkamp Stipend, the PEN Translation Fund, the Netherland America Foundation's Cultural Committee, the American Literary Translators Association (ALTA), the Austrian Ministry of Arts, and Norwegian Literature Abroad (NORLA). Thank you to Karen Emmerich and Princeton for having me as the Translator in Residence in 2020, and Merve Emre and Wesleyan for having me as a Distinguished Writer in Residence in 2023–24.

Special thanks to John Donatich, who commissioned this book and first suggested its title; to Abbie Storch and Ann-Marie Imbornoni, also at Yale University Press; and to the anonymous readers and other people who kindly read my work in progress: Esther Allen, Chris Clarke, Peter Cole, Madhu Kaza, Fred Neuhouser, and Paul Reitter.

INDEX

229